SIXTH-CENTURY ATHENS:
THE SOURCES

SOURCES IN ANCIENT HISTORY

General Editor: E. A. Judge, Macquarie University

This series is designed to provide translations of substantial bodies of source material with accompanying discussion particularly suitable for tutorial use by students of ancient history or of political and social institutions.

SIXTH-CENTURY ATHENS: THE SOURCES

A. FRENCH

SYDNEY UNIVERSITY PRESS

SYDNEY UNIVERSITY PRESS
Press Building, University of Sydney

UNITED KINGDOM, EUROPE, MIDDLE EAST, AFRICA
HB Sales, Littleton House, Littleton Road
Ashford, Middlesex TW15 1UQ, England

NORTH AND SOUTH AMERICA
International Specialized Book Services, Inc.
5602 N.E. Hassalo Street, Portland OR 97213-3640
United States of America

National Library of Australia Cataloguing-in-Publication data

French, A. (Alfred), 1916- .
Sixth-century Athens.

Bibliography.
Includes index.
ISBN 0 424 00123 3.

1. Athens (Greece)–History–Sources. 2. Greece–
History–Age of Tyrants, 7th-6th centuries, B. C. –
Sources. I. Title. (Series: Sources in ancient history)

938'.502

First published 1987
©A. French 1987

Printed in Australia by The Book Printer, Maryborough, Victoria

CONTENTS

AUTHOR'S NOTE

In preparing this book I had in mind the practical needs of students at the secondary or tertiary level who lack a sufficient knowledge of Classical Greek to work directly from the sources. In most cases the book will be used to best advantage in conjunction with a recommended history textbook, for example O. Murray, *Early Greece*, Fontana 1980, or V. Ehrenberg, *From Solon to Socrates*, Methuen 1973.

ABBREVIATIONS

ABSA	*Annual of the British School at Athens*
AJA	*American Journal of Archaeology*
AP	*Athenaion Politeia (The Constitution of Athens)* by Aristotle
FGH	F. Jacoby, *Die Fragmente der griechischen Historiker*
GHI	Meiggs and Lewis, *Greek Historical Inscriptions*
HAC	C. Hignett, *History of the Athenian Constitution*
HCT	A. W. Gomme, *A Historical Commentary on Thucydides*
JHS	*Journal of Hellenic Studies*

INTRODUCTION

The first three major episodes in Greek history about which we possess detailed information are all concerned with warfare – the Trojan War, of about 1200 BC; the Persian wars, about seven hundred years later; and the Peloponnesian War of 431–404 BC. The richness of information about some episodes, as compared with the poverty of knowledge about others, is strikingly reflected in the distribution of space allotted in modern history textbooks: almost as much space is allotted to the three or so years of the Persian conflict as is devoted to the whole of the preceding century. It is strange to think that we know more about the Trojan War (or rather, about the Trojan legend) than about any other single episode in Greek history until 480 BC.

The main reason for this very patchy coverage of the past is that detailed narratives of these three wars were fixed in a written account at an early stage (but in the case of the Trojan War several centuries after its occurrence). Not that accounts are necessarily to be trusted or believed merely because they are written down; and in the case of the Trojan War, few readers would accept as historical fact the Homeric saga, with its divine interventions, its trick miracles and its wide-screen heroics, although the classical Greeks seem to have taken the main lines of the narrative very seriously, and used its references as valid evidence in interstate disputes. A written account, unlike an oral tradition, provides an apparently firm framework of historical fact; once an episode has taken a written form, that account itself becomes the basis of future accounts, so that an inverted pyramid of historical writing springs from it.

Modern scholars who deal with early Athenian history have at their disposal the extant work of Greek historians who wrote in classical times, but in almost every case the writing is of events that took place more than a century before. In evaluating the historical value of such work scholars seek to trace back the sources on which the accounts of extant writers depend; that is, they seek the sources of the extant sources. Thus they are led back to the work of writers whose work is lost to us, but was available to the writers whose work survives; and occasionally we come into direct contact with the lost writers through quotation or reference in surviving work. There is a great mass of fragments of the work of Greek historians otherwise lost to us, and one of the triumphs of Greek historiography this century has been the collection and critical evaluation of these fragments, a task performed with immense erudition and in great depth by the German scholar, Felix Jacoby.[1] To him above all we are indebted for insight into the intricate interrelationships of the ancient sources.

We have no reason to doubt the statement of Thucydides (1.97.2) that his predecessors in historiography had confined themselves to writing about events just before the Persian War, or about that war itself. The sole exception whom he mentions was the writer Hellanicus of Lesbos, who wrote a brief chronicle of Athenian history from the earliest times until his own day, including a list of the early Athenian kings. Hellanicus lived on until late in the fifth century, as we know from the fact that he included in his work events from that era. We may therefore conclude that the earliest written history of Athens did not appear before the second half of the fifth century. Hellanicus could draw upon living witnesses for events as far back as the turn of the century, but for more or less the whole of the sixth century and beyond, he was dependent upon a chain of memory and hearsay. The first history of Athens to be written by a native Athenian was that of Cleidemus, who wrote in the mid-fourth century. His contemporary was the controversial historian Androtion, a public figure in his own right, and one of Aristotle's main sources. Among later historians of Athens was the much-quoted Philochorus, who wrote in the third century BC and was regarded as the author of a standard work.

What was the nature of the evidence on which Hellanicus and Cleidemus could draw for their account of early Athenian history? Without doubt their most important source was creative literature which had survived from that time; not written history, of course, but poetry. Like the sagas of Homer, the literature that survived from the seventh and sixth centuries was all in verse. This is not because the composition of verse necessarily precedes that of prose, but because a verse pattern enables a work to be memorized and transmitted from person to person in a set form, whereas the transmission of prose by oral communication involves a rephrasing, and often a reinterpretation, from speaker to speaker. Every version is different; only the theme remains constant, and even that varies in details, as we know from the many versions of a single story in folklore. Oral prose literature passes through many metamorphoses until it reaches a fixed form in writing; but verse literature is fixed from the start by its verse structure. The legends of the past, on which the first historians had to rely, preserved in many cases a genuine tradition, but were unreliable as a historical source because, like much folklore, they tended to be fanciful, exaggerated, partisan, and above all, careless in detail; their unreliability was demonstrated by the fact that different versions of the same event sometimes contradicted each

[1] *FGH.*

2

other. The verse texts, on the other hand, came to the historians, and through quotation have come down to us, more or less in the form in which they were first composed. The early poets whose work was available to the first historians included Solon of Athens, who came to be regarded by the ancients as a central figure in Athenian history.

The historians could congratulate fate on preserving for them a source of information so vital to their understanding of the past. Unfortunately, although the *text* of Solon's poems was relatively intact, and disputed at only a few points (regrettably some of them rather crucial), the problems of understanding it were great. Imaginative literature, especially the mystical and prophetic type composed by Solon, presents appalling problems of interpretation. We know what Solon *wrote* (or what the ancient writers believed that he wrote), but rarely can we be sure what he *meant*. The gap between what a poet says and what he means is notoriously wide, as we note even in the case of modern writers whose social and literary environment we share. Historians using poetry as a historical source have to look for realism in work heavy with symbolism and imagination. The ancient historians, like ourselves, found the expression and thought of Solon complex; by the fourth century his words had changed their meaning; the social context which appeared as the background to his verse contained elements that had long become obsolete. Modern critics, in trying to understand an old poem, will use their knowledge of the context to aid their understanding. Historians like Hellanicus and scholars like Aristotle had to try to discover the social context from the poetic text. A fair quantity of Solonian verse has come down to us through various sources, and we can compare the interpretation of his poems offered by the early Greek historians with our own understanding of the same passages. Hard indeed was the task of the first Greek historians in elucidating the meaning of their best source. And even if they could be sure that they did understand what Solon meant, what historian would care to accept without supporting evidence the account of a historical figure about his own achievement, and about his own place in history?

Greek writers who attempted to reconstruct the history of early Athens had at their disposal, apart from folklore and poetry, such family traditions as had been preserved by the descendants of aristocratic families, not without a certain regrooming and selectivity. The impact of family traditions as a source of knowledge is evident in the written history that emerges; the names of a few family groups crop up repeatedly, so that early Athenian history appears at times like the intermittent alliances and squabbles of these families. One has to decide whether the picture so appears merely because of the narrow range of information on which it rests, or whether this was indeed the true picture.

Ancient historians had also access to some public records. The years were officially numbered by the names of the chief magistrate at Athens (the eponymous archon), and a list of these chief magistrates was apparently common knowledge at Athens in the fifth century.[2] The actual laws of Solon were set up carved in wood, but later copies were made in stone: fragments of such copies were said to have been preserved into Roman times. Towards the end of the sixth century the practice of carving official documents on stone began to be a routine measure. Unfortunately most of the early records were lost when Athens was occupied by the Persians in 480-479. Archaeologists have found few inscriptions belonging to the sixth century, but some memorial and dedicatory inscriptions certainly survived into classical times, for there are references to them in literature. Thucydides himself, late in the fifth century, settled a historical dispute by quoting two early inscriptions, one a tomb epitaph, the other a dedication on an altar (6.54 and 59). Material objects, preserved for their value, both sentimental and financial, survived into classical, and even into modern times. They include fine metalwork, jewellery and heirlooms of various kinds which reveal a high level of craftsmanship and taste. But very little of the material environment of the old city survived into the fifth and fourth centuries. According to Herodotus (9.113) the Persian occupiers had refrained from extensive destruction of Athens' city, hoping to reach a settlement; but when Mardonius finally withdrew, he burned the city and demolished walls, buildings and monuments. When the Athenians returned, they found few houses and only parts of the city wall standing. Even these they themselves demolished in their frantic haste to build a new ring wall for defence (Thuc. 1.89). The city in which the fifth-century Athenians lived was a new town, linked to the old by sentiment and tradition; only legends reminded its inhabitants of the antiquity that they inherited. Psychologically the brash newness of their physical habitat cut them off from their past, making it more strange, and fertile in imaginative reconstruction.

About the middle of the fifth century, when the first history of Athens was being written, Herodotus of Halicarnassus was preparing his monumental work on the great confrontation of Greeks and Persians, a work of contemporary history, but including a number of episodes from earlier times to explain the causes of the clash. These episodes, which in the context of the great work count as mere digressions, included the fall

---

[1] Plato, *Hippias Major* 285E.

4

of the tyranny at Athens engineered by the Alcmaeonids, with a retrospect about their family curse; the internal struggle which followed the fall of the tyranny; the attempts of the Spartan king, Cleomenes, to foil the revolution; and finally, events which led to the decision of the Persians to restore the tyrant, Hippias. Herodotus' sources were oral, but his written account then took the place of the oral tradition and became itself the source on which later writers drew; Aristotle acknowledged him as a source, and Thucydides, without actually naming him, indicated quite clearly his knowledge of Herodotus' work. Occasional disagreements between Herodotus and Hellanicus indicate confusion in the oral tradition which was their common source; and Thucydides explicitly warned his readers of the unreliability of the oral traditions, giving examples of crude errors in beliefs even about contemporary matters (1.20).

Thanks to Herodotus, the story of the Athenian tyranny, brief and selective as it is, became the first long episode of known Athenian history. As regards earlier times, Herodotus knew the name of Solon, and he appears in his history, but it is as a Wise Man, the seer who warns the man of power (King Croesus) about the delusion of happiness and the snare of power. The legislation of Solon, and his place in Athenian constitutional development, was passed over by Herodotus with hardly a mention. Solon seems to have emerged on the stage of history as a man of action only late in the fifth century. It was after the oligarchic revolution, and amid the great controversy about the 'true ancestral constitution', that Solon was resurrected to become a subject of political debate. It was perhaps not until the fourth century, two hundred years after the event, that a written history which included an acount of Solon's reforms emerged, and Solon replaced Cleisthenes as the reputed founder of Anthenian democracy, an honour accorded only after the long controversy had succeeded in enveloping the whole question in a fog of confusion. This was the position when Aristotle, who had studied and worked at Plato's Academy, returned to Athens from Macedon: among the prodigious programme of research on which he embarked was a series of works on the constitutional development of several states, including Athens. How far the work was written by himself, or was merely supervised by him, remains a question of dispute; hence the modern habit of referring to the work as 'the *Constitution of Athens* by Aristotle, or "Aristotle" '. It was a compilation of research about the subject, based upon the reconstructions and interpretations of the fourth-century Attic historians (the so-called Atthidographers) liberally illustrated with quotations from the poems of Solon, but also drawing upon the work of Herodotus where relevant. Aristotle's book, which was concerned solely with the constitution, is the only history of Athens surviving from the fourth century, and it is not therefore surprising that the history of sixth-century Athens, of which Aristotle established himself as the major source, has appeared in later histories as a battleground of constitutional controversy, interrupted by the episode of the tyranny—a good-humoured interlude of Herodotean adventure in the epic style.

It was late in the nineteenth century when a copy of Aristotle's work, written on four rolls of papyrus, reached London from a site in Egypt, and immediately was accepted as the basic work on Athenian constitutional history, especially welcome because of its survey of the early period, about which so little was known. It aroused high hopes that at last light would shine into historical darkness. But the more closely it was examined, the greater appeared the difficulties of interpretation, caused by the controversial nature of Aristotle's sources, who had freely projected into the distant past their own ideological conflicts and political assumptions; and where the evidence had left gaps, they filled them with their own imaginative speculations.

Apart from the historical digressions of Herodotus and the constitutional reconstruction of Aristotle, we have inherited a source of information about the sixth century of a very different kind. During the first and second centuries AD, when the centre of power and wealth in the Mediterranean had shifted to Rome, Greek literature went through a period of classical revival. One of its more talented figures was the writer of essays and biographies, Plutarch, much of whose work has survived to the present day. He was a man of wide culture, with knowledge and experience of public affairs; his reading was extensive, and from a mass of material he composed both his *Moral Essays*, and his *Parallel Lives* of eminent Greeks and Romans. One of the subjects whom he selected for the latter series was Solon (the subject of the parallel Roman life was Publicola). Before the discovery of Aristotle's book, Plutarch's *Life of Solon* had been, for later historians, a mine of knowledge about the Athenian sixth century, and its imprint is still evident on modern history books. Its main interest lies in the fact that it preserves much written material known to Plutarch but unavailable to us.

Plutarch's biography of Solon was written more than six hundred years after the events with which it was concerned. The author lived in a minor province of the Roman empire at a time of political stability, in a political and social environment which was the result of centralized power and closely organized administration. It was a world which had accepted as a matter of course the existence of massive fortunes made from imperial exploitation and commercial development, far removed from the humble world of

Periclean Athens, let alone the far humbler world of sixth-century Greece. Plutarch was not a historian, but a literary artist: for his biographies and essays he selected from his wide reading whatever material seemed useful for his purposes, which were to illustrate and explain the background, achievements, and above all the *character* of his subjects. Since he took the whole of Greek and Roman history as the timeframe of his work, he was obviously not, nor did he claim to be, a specialist on any period: the range of authorities whom he cites is wide, and more or less undiscriminating, in the sense that he treats first-hand, second-hand or third-hand sources in much the same way, and mixes the comments of historians with those of popular writers. Students of history who wish to use Plutarch as a historical source should note his own criteria for the selection of material:

> It is not Histories that we are writing, but Lives; nor are the most famous deeds at all indicative of good or bad character, but often a trivial action or saying or piece of fun gives us a greater impression of a man's disposition than battles involving huge casualties . . .
> *Alexander*, ch.1

No one will object to the logic of Plutarch's statement; but for the understanding of sixth-century Athenian history it is the public actions of Solon that seem more relevant than his private disposition. Plutarch's particular approach meant that he did not regard as of major importance constitutional forms or legal niceties, so that he is not the best person to become the recorder of the legal system which tradition ascribed to Solon. Nor did chronology seem to Plutarch of excessive importance:

> About [Solon's] meeting with Croesus various writers have tried to prove that it was fictitious, on the grounds of chronology. But when a story is so famous and carried by so many authorities, and, more importantly, when it is so consistent with Solon's character, and bears the stamp of his wisdom and magnanimity, I cannot agree that it must be rejected on the so-called grounds of chronology, which so many writers have tried to revise, without any real success at resolving the difficulties.
>
> *Solon*, ch.27

Further doubts about Plutarch's historical sense and judgement are raised by his own views on the quality of Herodotus as a historian. In an attack upon the father of history Plutarch accused him of being a barbarian-lover, unfair in his treatment of Greek cities other than Athens, untruthful as regards facts, and faulty in judgement. Plutarch's attempt to write off Herodotus as a serious historian was part of a literary campaign which maligned the latter above all for his balance and fairness in presenting the clash between Greeks and Asians. To Plutarch history was primarily a song of praise in honour of great men.

Plutarch's *Life of Solon* fits into the general pattern of the series of *Lives*. Plutarch attempts a sketch of Solon's early life and background, about which little information remained except for references detected in Solon's own poems. Apart from the mainly trivial detail collected to pad out the *Life*, the material naturally centres upon the Solonian reforms, since it was that part of Solon's career that had been the subject of much of the writing available to Plutarch. The material that he recounts is more or less as in Aristotle, but it is enlivened with details inspired by various anecdotes which had collected about Solon, some of which are apparently included to show the cunning of the great reformer. Plutarch also includes his own surmises about Solon's motivation in his various acts: one such passage, which has been sometimes regarded by modern writers as an illuminating revelation, relates how Solon was concerned at the drift of population to Athens and the low productivity of the Attic countryside, which decided him to take measures to increase secondary industry and trade, and to punish idleness (ch.22). Plutarch also includes a list of measures otherwise unknown, such as one making illegal the sale of daughter or sister (unless she be shown to be no longer a virgin) (ch.23); a reform of the calendar, based on an interpretation of a verse in the *Odyssey* (ch.25); and intrusions into the realm of intimate private life by measures enforcing newly married couples to be shut into the bridal chamber, where they must eat together a quince, and requiring that the husband of an heiress should have sexual relations with her at least three times per month (ch.20). On questions of fact, Plutarch is not a reliable authority; and his speculations about motive should be examined critically. His knowledge of early Athenian history was limited, and his historical judgement was affected by the great difference between the world in which he lived and the ancient times about which he wrote, and into which he projected the conditions of modern history.

When historians choose to work in the field of prehistory they become dependent on their colleagues in archaeology to help them in many ways, especially chronology, by constructing from the surviving remains a sequence of the material culture of the people with whom they are concerned. In the case of Athens, the work of the archaeologists is hampered by the fact that almost the whole site of the ancient city is built over, and therefore out of reach of the excavator. But two areas, the Acropolis and the agora, have been available for investigation, and the results of the excavations are still under evaluation. Thucydides' remark (6.54.5) that the

Athenian tyrants 'beautified the city' implies that fine building took place in the sixth century; unfortunately the constructions would have been destroyed in the sack of Athens in 480–479, and incorporated in later building. Traces of such building have been found, but the chronology is difficult. There is however at least one impressive survival of grandiose construction, namely the foundations of the great temple of Zeus, reportedly begun during the tyranny and eventually completed in Roman times.

Of all the material evidence surviving from the sixth century none has aroused more interest or hope in the historian than that of the Athenian pottery, scattered over many sites, from Italy to the Black Sea area and the Near East: it is legitimate to expect that evidence about the state of Athenian manufacture, agriculture and trade may be gleaned from the clay containers in which the produce was transported. Athenian pottery was distinctive in style and can easily be identified (except that there were excellent foreign imitations, and some Athenian potters worked abroad), and tests of the clay can determine its origin. Thus the evidence of the pots can at least indicate lines of communication; or, perhaps, the terminals of communication. It has been possible to make some studies and plans of the distribution of Athenian wares, and the appearance of Athenian pots at sites where none had been found before shows a pattern of commercial expansion. On the basis of such studies it has been generally accepted that Athenian overseas trade considerably expanded during the sixth century, with implications for the development of city and ports, and for changes in the pattern of Athenian agricultural and industrial production.

Historians have accepted the implications of this evidence in some cases rather uncritically, and the limitations of the evidence need to be stressed. In the first place the final resting place of a container need not necessarily be its original destination: the pot could have been reused many times on many journeys, and could have carried the produce of other centres during its travels. The evidence as to lines of *communication* is sound; but this is very different from *patterns of distribution* of Athenian, or any other city's wares. The containers carried in a single ship which left an Attic port with produce from Attica could have been eventually scattered over areas which had no direct trading contacts with Athens. Secondly, there is often confusion in the statistics, between fine pottery (a luxury product) and simple containers for agricultural produce. The former may be grouped loosely together with other luxury commodities, such as jewellery, spices and precious objects which have, since the earliest times, been the subject of small-scale trading, and can prove very little about the economy of the trading partners. It is only the advent of bulk trading that is likely to change the shape of the economy, and it is primarily the traffic signalized by the containers that interests the economic historian. The evidence shows that there *was* bulk trading, and that some of it emanated from Athens. Unfortunately there is no chance of quantifying the trade: we can hope to make comparisons between the level of trade operating from different cities, and the rise or fall in the level of trade from a single city. But unless trade was a significant element in the economy, both comparisons are unhelpful. For if the place in the Attic economy occupied by the trade was below, say, 5 per cent of the gross product, a rise of a few per cent would make little discernible difference to the pattern of life. The theory of a great expansion in trade which changed Attica from an agricultural to a mixed, or a commercial, economy in the sixth century should be treated with caution. The theory has little support in the literary sources, apart from Plutarch, who viewed early Athens as passing through a stage similar to republican Rome, with a social struggle between patricians and plebeians and the rise of a mercantile group like the equestrians. The theory has commended itself to some modern historians in particular, because archaeology in this case seems to fill a gap in the record, a gap created because ancient historians were assumed not to understand economic history and to be uninterested in it. But the theory may have seriously exaggerated the importance of trade in early Athenian history.

The development of a significant trading centre in a geographical area implies the growth, or increase, of the use of money in that area to facilitate transactions. According to the literary tradition, at least three states of central Greece began to coin their own money during a period fixed in the literature by references to contemporary figures, including Pheidon of Argos and Solon of Athens, that is, to the seventh and early sixth centuries BC. Metallic coins are virturally indestructible, and all the metal yet minted is presumably still around, although most of the coins have been melted down for further uses. Coins are potentially among the most illuminating finds of archaeology, and a whole branch of history and archaeology devoted to numismatics has developed. The numismatists have arranged the finds of early coins in a satisfactory time sequence leading from the early electrum coins of Lydia to the silver owls of Athens. The start of the sequence has been anchored to the earliest identified group, buried under the base of the oldest building on the site of the temple of Artemis at Ephesus. We know approximately when the first temple on the site was *detroyed* (about the middle of the seventh century BC), so the date of its *construction* is not likely to be later than 700 BC. Since the coins had been in circulation before that time, their first usage could be dated to the eighth century. The earliest Greek coins are linked to the Lydian by imitation in technique and design, hence they follow them in the sequence, and have been dated to the seventh century, which fits well with the literary evidence. The first Athenian coinage, which is believed to follow that of Aegina and Corinth in the sequence, could fall into the era of the early sixth century, and the traditional connection of Solon with coinage in the 590s would thus appear quite plausible as far as the chronology goes.

The above is a very much simplified summary of the argument, but even so, the fragility of the reconstructed chronology is apparent. The gap between the invention of Lydian coinage and the sealing of the deposit in Ephesus, the gap between the Lydian invention and its spread to the Greek cities, and the gap between that time and the first coinage at Athens, are all based on guesswork, with a wide range of error due to unknown variables. It is accordingly not suprising that, over the last thirty years, the dates have all been disputed: an influential school of numismatists has established a different time sequence, claiming a date for the closing of the Ephesus deposit in the early sixth century, for the first electrum coins about 625 BC, and for the first Greek coins near the end of the seventh century. The adoption of this scheme renders the tradition that Solon adapted Athenian currency in the 590s implausible. Those who have accepted the numismatists' dating have been forced to choose between shifting Solon's legislation to the 570s, or else disconnecting the coinage tradition from Solon. The dispute continues; and a new time sequence may evolve.

Our knowledge of sixth-century Athenian history rests primarily on the surviving literary sources: the trustworthiness of the authorities on whom we depend can be no greater than the quality of the sources on which they, in their turn, depended. The archaeological evidence permits us direct contact with the material evidence of the ancient world, and is not dependent on the judgement or prejudice of a literary source. But the interpretation of the archaeological record is as difficult as that of the literary record, and conclusions based on the two disciplines sometimes point in different directions. The stage of early Athenian history is one on which many scenarios are possible, and the historian must decide at every point which scenario has the greatest probability of truth, in view of its authentication by evidence and its consistency with the total scene.

THE SOURCES

I THE FAILED COUP

The first event in Athenian history recalled by later historians of Athens concerns an abortive attempt to seize autocratic power, and the tragic consequences of its failure. These consequences included a massacre of the conspirators, involving a violation of sanctuary, and the exile of their murderers as men under a curse of blood guilt. The group was identified by tradition as the family of the Alcmaeonids (i.e the descendants of Alcmaeon), one of whose later descendants was Pericles. The story of the failed coup was perhaps unimportant in itself, but became a 'fact of history' when the mass of other material had long been forgotten, because the shadow of the curse laid upon the family group was brought up against the Alcmaeonids by their political opponents for generations to come, and was made to cast a sinister light on the personal careers and public roles of their distinguished descendants. The story first appears in the *History* of Herodotus, writing in the second half of the fifth century, that is two hundred years after the event. The story was repeated, with some added details, by Thucydides, writing near the end of the fifth century.

(a) The way in which the Alcmaeonids came to be known as the 'accursed of Athens' was as follows. Cylon of Athens was an Olympic champion[1] who aimed to set up a tyranny. He collected a group of accomplices, and attempted to seize the Acropolis. When his attempt failed, he sought sanctuary at the foot of the statue. The presidents of the naucraries,[2] who administered Athens in those days, raised them up under guarantee that their lives would be spared. But the blame for their subsequent slaughter is laid upon the Alcmaeonids. All this happened before the time of Peisistratus.

Herodotus 5.71

---

1. The reference to the Olympic victory is important in dating the massacre. A list of Olympic victors, dating back to the inauguration of the festival, existed in classical times, and according to this list Cylon's victory was placed in the 35th Olympiad, that is, in 640 BC. Whether the list was in fact accurate is uncertain, and doubts have been cast upon its authenticity on the grounds that the evidence on which it was compiled was dubious, and also because of the uncertainty about whether the festival was, in its early stages, an annual one

14

or, as in historical times, fell every fourth year; even if the compiler had a correct list of victors in the correct order of their victories there still might remain a doubt about the years to which they should be assigned. (The argument may give some insight into the enormous problems of determining an exact chronology for early Greek history.) Most modern historians accept the date 640 for the victory, and assume that the attempted coup followed shortly afterwards.

2. The question of who was ultimately responsible for the sacrilege came to have grave consequences in public life; it is accordingly not surprising that alternative answers were offered. Herodotus preserves a tradition, denied by Thucydides (see below), that the chief officials at Athens at the time were the presidents of the naucraries, about whom we know almost nothing, except that, according to Aristotle *(Constitution of Athens,* ch.8, later referred to as *AP*), they were in early times responsible for certain financial offices. The other tradition, carried by Thucydides, assumes that the archons were then the chief magistrates. The question is important for the correct placing of guilt for the massacre, as Megacles, the Alcmaeonid, was chief archon at the time.

(b) In earlier times there lived an Athenian, Cylon, an Olympic champion, of high birth and considerable influence: he had married the daughter of Theagenes of Megara, who at that time was the tyrant[1] of that city. When Cylon consulted the oracle at Delphi, he received an answer from the god that he should seize the Acropolis of Athens at the great festival of Zeus. Cylon managed to get from Theagenes a task force, and persuaded friends to join him; when the Olympic festival in the Peloponnese took place, he seized the [Athenian] Acropolis with a view to setting up a tyranny, under the impression that this was what was meant by the 'great festival of Zeus', and that its relevance was to the fact that he was an Olympic victor . . . . So he made his attempt, believing that he had made the correct interpretation. But when the Athenians realized the situation, they came pouring in *en masse* from the country to stop him, and settled down to besiege him. With the passage of time they tired of the blockade, and most of them withdrew, handing over responsibility for the blockade to the nine archons, and giving them a free hand to take whatever action they thought best (in those days it was the archons who carried most responsibility for administrative affairs[2]). Pinned down by the blockade, and running short of food and water, Cylon's group was now in dire straits, when he and his brother made their escape. When the rest of them were desperate, and some were dying of hunger, they sought sanctuary on the altar of the Acropolis.

When the Athenians on guard duty saw that men were dying in the temple, they gave them a hand, and took them out under condition of safe conduct: they then put them to death. On the way out some prisoners took refuge on the altars of the Holy Ones, and were executed there. This, then, is the incident which resulted in that family being called 'accursed', and an abomination in the sight of the Goddess, both they and their descendants after them. Accordingly these men were driven out of the country, as polluted, by the Athenians on that occasion, and later on by the Spartan Cleomenes and an Athenian faction. The living were exiled; the bones of the dead were collected and cast out. However, at a later stage they returned, and their kin live in Athens to this day.[3]

Thucydides 1.126

---

1. The terms 'tyrant' and 'tyranny' were used in classical times to refer to autocratic regimes usually set up by an act of usurpation and the suspension of lawful government, that is, government in accordance with the traditional constitution. The term 'tyrant' was an alien one, and, at least as applied to the early Greek tyrannies, very difficult to define, as it generally referred to *illegal*, or *unofficial* officials, with no fixed powers or privileges, or even titles, except the title attributed to them by critics. Tyrannies first appeared in Greece in the seventh and sixth centuries, always at centres of urban development and inter-state commerce, so that a link with economic change is often assumed, but cannot be clearly established. It may be said with reasonable safety that tyrannies occurred at times and places of social conflict which involved economic change, resulting in the temporary, or permanent, breakdown of the established social order, and the evolution of new conditions. Theagenes was believed to have been tyrant at Megara, Athens' western neighbour, in the second half of the seventh century.
2. The narrative suggests that Thucydides had read, and was following, that of Herodotus, but that Thucydides chose to correct him at this point. The archons were not the chief officials at Athens in his own time, nor in that of Herodotus, but Thucydides believed that they had been in the late seventh century, and in this he seems to have been followed by Aristotle, *AP* 13.
3. That is, in the late fifth century.

II SOCIAL CRISIS IN MEGARA

During the seventh and sixth centuries BC a form of lyric poetry, very realistic in style and content, evolved in Ionia and the islands. A considerable body of this poetry has been preserved, and, used with appropriate caution, can shed light on contemporary social conditions outside Athens. There are many references in the verses of Alcaeus of Lesbos to civic strife, the storms that beat upon the ship of state, tyranny, and exile. The following passage is attributed to Theognis, a poet of Athens' neighbour Megara, writing in the sixth century. (Megara in fact was ruled by a tyrant in the seventh century, see I(b) n.1).

My friend, this city is pregnant, and I fear may bring forth
a man to bring retribution for our wicked violence.
The city folk are sound; but the chiefs
are transformed and set to fall into dire calamity.
No city yet, my friend, was ever wrecked by goodly men,
but only when base elements decide to run amok.
They corrupt the populace, grant rights to the unrighteous
to advance their own power and wealth.
Do not expect that such a city will endure for long unshaken,
though all be peaceful yet,
while base men's appetites are whetted
by wealth, which brings in train collective tragedy.
From such things grow civic strife, communal bloodshed,
and one-man rule. May our city be spared such a fate!

          . . .

The city still abides, but changed the folk!
Men who once knew neither justice nor laws,
wore goatskins on their backs
and dwelt like beasts outside the town,
they now are high and mighty, and those
once exalted, now are fallen low . . .

Theognis 39–58

The message of the poem seems to be: 'Our nobility, corrupted by wealth, are heading for disaster. In their blindness they flirt with sinister elements in society, sharing their power and rights with unworthy people. Rabble from the countryside, with little conception of law and justice, are challenging the traditional rule of the aristocracy. Such confusion can lead to the overthrow of lawful government, and usurpation by an autocrat.'

The picture of turbulent social conditions agrees substantially with that which may be inferred from other verse of the time and the poems are in any case of great interest as literary sources shedding light on conditions more or less contemporary to the writers. But the difficulties and perils of coaxing conclusions about social history from such poems are obvious:

only the most general statements can be hazarded, but even these may help in attempting to put together a historical scenario based mainly on the poems of Solon, as requoted and interpreted by later Greek scholars.

III SOLON OF ATHENS

Herodotus in his *History* introduces Solon in an anecdote whose point is to illustrate how a great ruler can bring about his own fall by his infatuation with success and power, although he had been warned by a wise man. Croesus was king of Lydia during the years 560–547, and since the date conventionally assigned to Solon's period of office in Athens was 594 BC (Diogenes Laertius 1.62), and his period of overseas travel therefore between 594 and 584, there seems to be something wrong with the chronology.

At a time when Croesus had added these conquests to the Lydian realm there came to Sardis, then at the height of its prosperity, all the Wise Men of Greece of that epoch. Among them, in particular, came Solon of Athens, who had drafted laws for the Athenians at their request, and had then gone abroad for ten years. Ostensibly, it was to see the world; in fact it was to avoid a position in which he might be forced to repeal any of the laws he had made. This was because the Athenians were unable to do such a thing themselves, as they had bound themselves by solemn oaths to recognize as valid for ten years the body of law that Solon should give them.

Herodotus 1.29

The chief interest of the anecdote for historians is not so much the truth, or otherwise, of the details given by Herodotus, as the insight given into the reputation of Solon at Athens in the mid-fifth century as one of the recognized Sages of antiquity, and a lawgiver. The fact that Herodotus does not refer to Solon's later reputation as an economic reformer and as the founder of Athenian democracy may be, and has been, taken to imply that such a reputation was unknown to Herodotus at the time, and was mainly the creation of later writers. In Book 6.131 he describes Cleisthenes as 'the man who gave the Athenians their tribes and the democracy'.

IV THE PROPHECY OF SOLON

About the middle of the fourth century BC the orator Demosthenes, in
a speech for the prosecution, quotes Solon, apparently to recall the horror
with which the Wise Man of antiquity regarded dishonesty in public life.
The quotation is incomplete, with some gaps, and the text is at points
disputed (line 22, printed between asterisks below, can scarcely be said to
make sense, and editors have made efforts, without much success, to make
sense of it).

Please read out these elegiac verses of Solon, so you may see that Solon
too despised men of that type:

> Never will ruin fall upon our city by the verdict of Zeus
> or by the will of the blessed, the deathless gods,
> such a guardian we have, great-hearted, of mighty parentage,
> Pallas Athene, who holds above us her sheltering hands.
> 5 It is the citizens themselves who, in their folly,
> led on by material gain, threaten to destroy our city,
> and the mind of the people's leaders is unrighteous.
> For them awaits the endurance of many sufferings, the fruit of
>   great hubris.
> For they know not how to check their wanton greed, nor enjoy in
>   peace
> 10 the blessing of feasts that lie before them.
>
> . . .
>
> they enrich themselves, led on by unrighteous deeds
>
> . . .
>
> sparing neither sacred nor communal property,
> robbers, they loot on all sides,
> and brush aside the holy commandments of Justice.
> 15 But She in silence marks what is done, and what has come to pass,
> and comes assuredly in the fullness of time to exact retribution—
> thus inevitable catastrophe is coming upon the whole city,
> as it slides into base servitude—
> She who awakens civic strife and sleeping war,
> 20 war that destroys the comely youth of many men,
> for it is by enemy hands that our beloved city
> * is blighted in confrontations where they wrong loyal men*.

19

Such are the evils rife among the people; and of the poor
many journey on their way to a foreign land,
25 sold and fettered with humiliating bonds.

. . .

thus comes the communal misfortune home to every one,
no longer can his hall's gates hold it back,
though the barrier be high, assuredly it finds him out
though he shrink and cower in his innermost room.
30 This, then, is what my heart bids me tell to the Athenians —
that Lawlessness above all brings ruin on a city,
but Good Order brings harmony, makes all things straight,
puts bonds upon offenders,
smooths out what is harsh, checks gross excess, bridles hubris,
35 withers the budding blooms of blind recklessness,
makes crooked judgements straight, humbles the works
of violence, ends the works of discord,
ends the bitterness of harsh contention. Beneath Her rule
the realm of man is filled with sanity and wisdom.

Gentlemen, you hear what Solon has to say about such men, and about
the gods who, as he says, preserve our city.

Demosthenes, *The Corrupt Delegation*, chs 254–6

The general sentiments of the poem — the dangers of violence, outrage,
and injustice, especially in high places, and the inevitable retribution — are
traditional, and are echoed, for instance, in Hesiod's *Works and Days* (lines
213–24), and by Solon himself in the poem quoted by Stobaeus, *Eclogues*
3.9: hubris, overweening pride, accompanied by infatuation, brings its own
nemesis. Not content with their present blessings, the leaders, says Solon,
are led by their material greed to act like brigands, trampling upon the
sanctions imposed by holy and common law: examples of their victims are
humble men, sold, fettered, and exiled. From such evil works comes strife
and war; the city is sinking into servitude. Such are the fruits of
unrighteousness. And the remedy? Good order, *eunomia* (which was
incidentally the word applied to the traditional Spartan system of
government), will restore harmony and peace. Solon's message to Athens
is the need to restore the rule of law, and respect for traditional values.

Historians have treated the verses as an occasional poem on the current
problems of Athens. But the general theme is poetic, symbolic, and timeless:

it illustrates well the type of gnomic wisdom for which Solon was celebrated, and supports the picture of Solon left by Herodotus (1.29.34) in his anecdote of the meeting of the king and the philosopher. Obviously, to extract from such a poem references to actual contemporary situations is difficult and liable to grotesque misunderstandings. Much has been made of lines 23–5, often quoted out of context. They have been taken as evidence supporting Aristotle's theory that a social crisis had been caused, at least in part, by the enslavement of peasants for debt, in accordance with a law of Dracon, later repealed by Solon. The interpretation is attractive, and may have influenced Aristotle himself. On the other hand Solon, if we are to take him literally, seems to be concerned not by the harshness of the legal system in force but by the *lack* of legality: he charges the leaders with behaving like brigands, disregarding the laws of god and man. The reference to fetters in line 25 (a reference which is universally taken to be literally meant), is answered, in line 33, by another reference which is perhaps symbolic: 'Now it is the down-trodden peasants who are fettered: on the day of reckoning it will be the true offenders'. A further problem is the reference in line 18 to the community sinking into servitude. Here the servitude is apparently symbolic, and has nothing to do with enslaving peasants: the whole community is affected; its downfall is like that of a man who loses his freedom. Taken together with the reference to war, in line 19, it might be taken to refer literally to the danger of defeat and enslavement for the Athenians, perhaps in the war with Megara for Salamis. (It is possible, in fact, that this is what Demosthenes thought the poem referred to, when he quoted it.) One must always bear in mind that Solon was a *poet*, and it is not easy to extract from writings which are the product of his poetic imagination (as well as the product of the world he lived in) a profile of Solon, the statesman.

V ARISTOTLE'S RECONSTRUCTION OF THE CRISIS IN EARLY ATTICA

In the late fifth century political controversy about the 'traditional constitution' of Athens and the origin of Athenian democracy drew attention to the historical role of Solon as a lawgiver, and led scholars to scrutinize the tradition about him. This tradition was, apart from the poems attributed to him, derived from the store of belief about the past, which had been preserved in the memory of men and handed down from generation to generation with inevitable refinements, omissions and accretions. In trying to establish the truth about Solon, a scholar like Aristotle could refer to fifth-century histories, which had attempted to fix in writing the oral traditions available, and could reread the poems in the light of such books. He could also attempt to discover, from the laws still in operation and attributed to Solon, the aims of such laws, and the social problems with which they had tried to deal. In attempting such a task of reconstruction Aristotle was handicapped by the obscurity of the poems; by the fact that there was not agreement which of the laws *were* originally Solonian; and because of the general ignorance about conditions in Attica in Solon's time. It was impossible for Aristotle to know how far he could be misled by applying to this early period theoretical models of social and political conditions derived from his own time. It is thus with appropriate caution that his reconstruction of the situation at Athens about 600 BC is to be read.

(a) The nobles and commons had been feuding for some time. The whole political set-up at Athens was oligarchic;[1] in particular the poor, together with wives and children, had come to be in bondage to the rich, and were known as 'dependants' (*pelatae*) and 'sixth-parters' (hectemoroi);[2] for it was on this basis that they worked the land of the rich. (All the land was now in the possession of the few.) If they failed to render their dues, they and their children became liable to seizure. (All loans were contracted upon the security of the person until Solon's time: he it was who became the first 'champion of the people'.) The hardest and most bitter feature of the system for the masses was the incidence of enslavement; not that this was their only grievance, for they were more or less without any say at all in public affairs.

Aristotle, *AP* 2

---

1. The terminology used is that of Aristotle's time. The conflict is portrayed as one between the democrats and the oligarchs, the many and the few: the term 'champion of the people', that is, of the popular cause, was a term applied in the fifth century to the leader of the democrats. The difficulty of applying these 'modern' terms to Solon's time without misrepresenting the situation is apparent from Aristotle's own account. In classical times democrats and oligarchs were rival factions within the citizen body; they were in general agreement about the participatory style of government, but disagreed about how wide or narrow should be the body which exercised political control. But, in Aristotle's account, the division appears as between noble landowners and enslaved peasants. Terminology derived from later party politics in an urban environment is transferred to an earlier period and to a rural environment, where, at first sight, the situation

appears as the prelude to a threatened slave rising.

2. The terms *pelatae* and *hectemoroi* had survived, but their exact meaning had apparently been forgotten, and Aristotle feels it necessary to explain the latter term. His definition may be based on nothing more than his idea of its etymology, and has not been universally accepted. (Some modern historians have claimed that the term implies that the dependant surrendered five-sixths of his produce and kept one-sixth: but for a peasant to survive, with a family, on one-sixth of his product, the latter would presumably have to be so extraordinarily high that it is difficult to see why he would ever have fallen into debt in the first place, assuming that debt is the origin of his condition.) Aristotle's reconstruction is based on the belief that debts and land mortgages were at the heart of the Attic rural crisis: we shall examine later (Section VI) the basis for this belief. Modern historians have suggested alternative, or additional, possible causes for the growth of slave or bonded labour in Attica. It is possible, for example, that land which had gone out of cultivation in the Dark Age or the eighth century, during conditions of unusual drought, had been resettled by rich men with bonded labour brought into the area (the *hectemoroi*).

(b) Such was the political order, with the majority in a state of enslavement to the minority, when the demos confronted the notables. The civic strife was severe; and they had been ranged against each other for some time when they chose by agreement, as mediator and archon, Solon; and they put the constitution into his hands.

AP 5.1

(c) After being put in charge of affairs, Solon liberated the demos, in the present and for the future, by prohibiting all lending on the security of the person. He also passed laws; and brought about the cancellation of debts, both private and communal; which cancellations are termed the *seisachtheia*, meaning that they 'shook off their burdens'.

AP 6.1

According to the reconstruction of Aristotle, peasant indebtedness had caused the enslavement of poor farmers. Solon solved the problems at one stroke by cancelling all the debts and restoring land and freedom to the peasants, and ensured that the situation would not recur by passing a law that henceforth no debt could be contracted on personal security.

(d) These then were the democratic aspects of the [new] legal code. It was before this legislation that Solon brought about the cancellation of debts, and, after it, an increase in measures, weights, and coins. Under Solon the measures [of capacity] were made larger than the Pheidonian type; and the mina, which previously had been equivalent in weight to 70 drachmas, was now brought up to 100. (The earlier coin had been the two-drachma piece.) Solon also brought in the [system of] weights corresponding to the coins, making the talent the equivalent of 63 minas, the three [extra] minas being distributed between the stater and the other denominations.

AP 10

Aristotle began that section of the *AP* dealing with the work of Solon by a discussion of the sources of the crisis (ch. 5); continued with a brief note on the cancellation of debts and prohibition of future loans on personal security (ch. 6); then, in chapters 7–9, he discussed the constitutional legislation attributed to Solon. In chapter 10 Aristotle interrupted this unfinished discussion by reverting, in the above note, to economic matters. By this arrangement of the material he seems to be emphasizing what he believed to be the sequence of actions: first came the cancellation of debts, followed by the legislation, and *only then* came the changes in the weights, measures and coins. The conscious separation (in the narrative) of debt cancellation from changes in the weights can be attributed to Aristotle's wish to refute a theory advanced by Androtion (unmentioned by Aristotle, but cited by Plutarch, see below) that Solon did *not* cancel debts, but helped the indebted peasants by a less controversial method, which included alterations to the official measures and coinage. (For discussion of the plausibility of Androtion's theory see below.)

Aristotle attributed to Solon responsibility for Athens' adoption of the standard of weights, measures and coins used in 'modern' times. In his view the Athenians earlier used a standard of weights corresponding to that attributed to a early shadowy figure, Pheidon of Argos, a standard in use later in Aegina and parts of the Peloponnesus. Solon was supposed to have somehow switched Athenian usage to a different standard, corresponding to that used in Corinth and Euboea. Talent and mina were terms both of weight and currency value. Aristotle refers to a change in the relationship between the mina and the drachma, and in his account it is not entirely clear whether he believed that the mina remained constant in weight and the drachma was made lighter (as the same quantity of silver was divided into a larger number of coins), or conversely the drachma retained its weight and the mina was made heavier. In Androtion's theory, as quoted by

Plutarch, the former alternative is implied ('Debtors repaid their debts, contracted in the old, heavier, and consequently more valuable drachmas, by the same number of lighter drachmas'). Aristotle complicates his account by mentioning another change, affecting principally the relation between the mina and the talent. A talent, as bullion, still weighed 60 minas, but was the equivalent in value to 63 minas worth of drachmas: thus to the extent that the drachma was undervalued by 5 per cent, presumably to cover the cost of minting, it assumed a quality of token coinage.

This appears to be what Aristotle means. Difficulty in understanding it stems not so much for the nature of the material as from the fact that Aristotle's comment is so very brief and simplified; and that is because he was concerned, not so much with a discussion of the changes in themselves, as to emphasize that, although he accepted that there *were* changes in the currency etc., the changes were unrelated to the *seisachtheia*, in spite of Androtion's claim.

It is a different question altogether whether tradition was correct in attributing changes in the currency to Solon, and why he should have made such changes. Some modern historians, accepting the attribution to Solon, have credited him with a far-sighted policy of state planning for commercial expansion – linking Athens to the Corinthian market and the western Greek colonies in Italy and Sicily. But the whole idea of the sixth-century poet-lawgiver conceiving such plans seems rather romantic. In recent times what appeared to be a stunning blow was struck to the whole theory by the claim of numismatists that the first Athenian coinage did not in any case appear before about 575 BC, and therefore could only be credited to Solon if the dating for his reforms were shifted to that later period, a solution accepted by some historians. But more recently a rather cogent case has been made for the view that the numismatists themselves are on shaky ground in their revised dating, and the first Athenian coinage may, after all, be earlier than they have alleged. The issue of dating remains unresolved.

For further reading see C. M. Kraay, 'An interpretation of *Ath. Pol.* ch. 10' in *Essays in Greek coinage presented to Stanley Robinson*, Oxford 1968, 1–9; L. Weidauer, *Probleme der frühen Elektronprägung*, Freiburg 1975; D. Kagan, 'The dates of the earliest coins', *AJA* 86, 1982, 343–60; J. H. Kroll and N. M. Waggoner, 'Dating the earliest coins of Athens, Corinth and Aegina', *AJA* 88, 1984, 293–304.

VI PLUTARCH ON THE CRISIS

Plutarch's narrative evidently owes much to Aristotle, and sometimes follows him almost word for word. But whereas Aristotle had dismissed the theory of the fourth-century historian Androtion by implication, and without quoting it, Plutarch spells the theory out, only to reject it likewise. In agreeing with Aristotle that the *seisachteia* was indeed a total cancellation of debts, Plutarch quotes from Solon verses which appear to clinch this view. In fourth-century Attica it was possible for land to be offered as security against debt, and land thus pledged was marked by a *horos*, a marker stone advertising that a legal encumbrance lay on the land. More than one hundred such inscribed *horoi* have been found in Attica, none referring to a time earlier than the fourth century. When Solon wrote that he lifted the *horoi* and freed the land, it thus appeared that he was referring to the fact that he had cancelled the debts, and consequently the pledges which marked the debts.

(a) At that time the disparity between rich and poor had reached a peak. The situation of Athens had become precarious in the extreme, and it seemed that only through the establishment of a tyranny could a way be found to achieve stability and put an end to conflict. The whole of the demos was in debt to the rich; either they worked the land of the latter rendering to them one-sixth of the produce (they were known as *hectemoroi* or *thetes*), or else, after incurring debts on their own personal security, they were liable to seizure by their creditors: some stayed on as slaves, others were sold abroad. Many were even forced to sell their own children, for there was no law against it, and to flee from their own country because of the ruthlessness of the creditors.

The majority, however, and the toughest characters among them, began to combine forces. They encouraged each other not to tolerate the situation but to choose a single leader, someone they could trust; to liberate the foreclosed debtors; to redivide the land; and to make a clean sweep of the whole system.

It was now that the shrewdest of the Athenians turned to Solon, as one person at least who was not compromised in the blunders that had been made: he had played no part in the misdeeds of the rich, nor had he been involved in the privations of the poor. They begged him to come forward publicly, and bring the conflict to an end.

Phanias of Lesbos however writes that Solon chose to play a trick on both sides in the interests of the salvation of Athens. He secretly promised to the deprived a redistribution of land, and to the rich an enforcement of contracts. Solon however recalls the reluctance with which he entered the public arena, fearing the rapacity of one party and the recklessness of the other. He was elected archon in succession to Philombrotos, and simultaneously to be mediator and lawgiver, being readily accepted by the rich as a man of substance, and by the poor as an honest broker.

Plutarch, *Solon* 13–14

(b) Modern writers note the Athenian habit of disguising the unpleasant aspect of things by the use of nice and charitable euphemisms, thus urbanely glossing over the reality. They refer to whores as 'escorts', taxes as 'subscriptions', occupation troops as 'public security', and gaol as 'the nick'. Solon, it seems was a pioneer of this form of wit, when he termed the annulment of people's debts 'the *seisachtheia*' (or 'discharge of burdens'). For this was his first public act, when he announced that all existing debts were annulled, and that in future there should be no lending on personal security. Some writers, however, including Androtion, have maintained that Solon relieved the poor not by any cancellation of debts but by a reduction of interest, and that in their delight they gave the name of the *seisachtheia* to this humane act, and also to the accompanying enlargement of the measures, and the value of the currency. For whereas the mina had previously weighed 70 drachmas, he now made it equivalent to 100. Thus repayment was made equivalent [to the indebted sum] reckoned in the number of coins, but lesser in value, which meant a substantial bonus for the payers, without involving any loss to those they paid. Most authorities, however, say that the *seisachtheia* was the cancellation of all the contracts; and the poems are more consistent with this view. For Solon, in the following verses, prides himself on the fact that, from the pledged land

he lifted the *horoi*, driven in at many points:
before, She was in bondage, now She is free . . .

and of those citizens who had become liable to seizure for money, some he brought home from abroad

. . . speaking no more the Attic tongue
in their manifold wanderings abroad,
and others who endured humiliating servitude
at home . . .

he set them free, he says.

Plutarch, Solon 15

A connection between the lifting of the *horoi* and the cancellation of debts had already been made by Aristotle, who quoted from the same poem:

With reference to the cancellation of debts and the liberation by the *seisachtheia*, of those previously enslaved [Solon wrote]:

> Of the aims for which I had called together the demos,
> which did I leave unattained?
> Be my best witness before the judgement of time,
> the great mother of the Olympian spirits,
> black Earth, she from whom
> I lifted the *horoi*, driven in at many points:
> before, She was in bondage, now She is free . . .

Aristotle, AP 12.4

The word *horos* was used in Greek from Homer onwards in the sense of a 'border marker', and by coincidence Solon himself used it in this sense, when he wrote:

> I stood like a *horos* in the middle ground
> between them . . .

AP 12.5

But in the fourth century the word had taken on the additional meaning, denoting a 'mortgage stone' set on land pledged as security for debt, and carrying the details of the pledge. It is possible, but unlikely, that this was an ancient use of the term; but we must at least bear in mind the possibility that the word obtained the 'modern' meaning only when the use of land for security against debt is known to have begun, that is, in the later period. We cannot by any means exclude the possibility that, in his reference to 'lifting the stones', that is the border markers, Solon was not referring to 'mortgages' or debts at all, but to the reuniting of land that had previously been wrongly divided, for example communal pasture which had been illegally enclosed, or private property which had been confiscated, divided and sold when a family group (the Alcmaeonids?) had been driven into exile.

Of course, such possibilities must have been apparent to fourth-century scholars too, but they chose to understand Solon's use of the term *horos* in the contemporary sense: it confirmed (if it did not actually inspire) the theory of debt as the basic cause of the crisis. It is remarkable that although Aristotle quoted liberally from Solon as his only primary source to support his reconstruction of events, there is nevertheless no unambiguous reference to debt in any of his quotations, nor in any extant verses of Solon preserved elsewhere. This statement may be challenged, for there is one line in which a reference to debt has indeed been detected. Aristotle is quoting Solon:

> Many men I brought home to divine-built Athens,
> men who had been sold, some without justice,
> some justly; and others had fled abroad
> *under dire constraint*, speaking no more the Attic tongue,
> in their manifold wanderings abroad,
> and others who endured humiliating servitude
> at home, trembling before the whim of masters;
> I set them free.
>
> *AP* 12

The phrase above translated as *under dire constraint*, which is itself an echo from Homer, has sometimes been translated as 'under dire constraint of debts', or as 'because of debts arising from necessity'. The text is disputed at this point, and appears in two different forms in the two existing copies. For a historian it is hard to base an argument on the interpretation of a disputed text: it is enough to indicate how precarious is the theory advanced by Aristotle, resting as it does to a considerable extent on the interpretation of two phrases in Solon, which are themselves the subject of controversy.

Of course, the fact that a historical reconstruction appears to rest upon precarious foundations does not mean that it is wrong. But the student of history should be aware of both the limitations of the primary evidence, and the limitations imposed upon scholars like Androtion, Aristotle and Plutarch by the state of knowledge and the intellectual environment of their time, so that the plausibility of their accounts can be seen in perspective.

Concerning the plausibility of Androtion's theory, that the *seisachtheia* consisted not in the cancellation of debts but in the reduction of the rate of interest and changes to the currency, modern historians in general agree with Aristotle, Plutarch, and the majority of Plutarch's sources in rejecting it. Androtion's view, that the currency change helped the debtors without harming the creditors (who received back less silver than they had loaned), certainly appears eccentric and improbable. Furthermore the theory assumes that the rural debts were (like those on the fourth-century *horoi*) expressed in money terms, and that rural Attica, at the time when the debts were incurred, operated on a money economy; whereas in fact most of the debts would probably in any case have been expressed in kind. And incidentally, the increase in the measures of capacity would surely have, in that case, benefited the *creditor* (who would have received back the same number of (larger) measures) and harmed the *debtor*. Modern historians have attributed to Androtion a political motive for his theory, namely a desire to protect Solon from the taint of revolutionary politics, typified by such a radical measure as the cancellation of debts. From Plutarch's amusing note on the Athenian practice of using euphemisms to disguise unpleasant acts, it is clear that he, in the context of his own time, regarded the cancellation of debts as a social policy both unpalatable and dangerous.

The disagreement between Androtion and his critics about the meaning of the *seisachtheia*, and the exact force of Solon's law, could, one may assume, easily have been settled once and for all, without the need to discuss its economic plausibility, by consulting the actual law, if it was available for inspection. Plutarch writes (*Solon* 24, see Section VII(c)) as if copies of Solon's laws were in fact available in fourth-century Athens. The fact that there was no attempt to refute Androtion by reference to the terms of the law would seem to tell against this view.

VII   OTHER ECONOMIC MEASURES

Solon has been credited by some modern historians with a wide-ranging policy of economic development for Athens, inclining her on to a path of industrialization and commercial growth. The economy was to be diversified by the active encouragement of crafts, alien craftsmen were to be encouraged to settle permanently in Athens, and foreign traders were to be attracted to Athenian ports by the offer of exports: at the same time (by an apparent contradiction) food was to be retained in the country by the prohibition of all food exports except oil. This theory rests not on the evidence of Solon's poems, nor on Aristotle's interpretation of them, but mainly on references in Plutarch's *Life of Solon*.

(a) The idea that a relatively even distribution in the pattern of land ownership had an important bearing upon the political structure was clearly understood by some, even in the distant past. There was, for instance, the law of Solon, also paralleled elsewhere, which set limits to the amount of land any individual could acquire.

Aristotle, *Politics* 1266b, 17–19

(b) Solon noted that the city [of Athens] was filling up with the people who were constantly streaming into Attica from all quarters because of the security of conditions there. He realized at the same time that most of the country was of poor quality and low yield, and that those who sail the seas are not in the habit of bringing goods to those who have nothing to offer in exchange. Solon therefore switched the attention of the Athenians towards the trades, and passed a law that there should be no obligation upon a son to maintain his father if the latter had omitted to teach him a trade. . . . Solon, who observed that the land [of Attica] barely produced a subsistence for those who worked it, and was incapable of supporting an idle, feckless mob, raised the prestige of the trades, and instructed the Council of the Areopagus to scrutinize everyone's means of livelihood, and to punish the idlers.

Plutarch, *Solon* 22

(c) As for the products of the earth Solon permitted only olive oil to be disposed of to foreigners, and he prohibited the export of all other products. In the case of any who did so export, Solon directed the archon to put a curse upon them, unless the offender paid a hundred drachmas into the public treasury. It is the first *axon* (tablet) which carries this law. . . . Very perplexing is the law on naturalization, for it permits the grant of citizen rights only to those permanently exiled from their own country, or else those who have emigrated to Athens with their families to practise a trade.

Plutarch, *Solon* 24

The references to Solon's preoccupation with economics may seem more significant when grouped together out of context, but they form only a part of a mass of anecdotes about Solon, some of which test the credibility of Plutarch himself. It is, however, his policy to pass on all relevant material, sometimes giving the source of his knowledge, even though he may suspend belief himself about it. Among the laws, or ideas, ascribed to Solon in Plutarch's account are, for instance: a law permitting the remarriage of an heiress to a kinsman of her husband if he proves incapable of exerting his conjugal rights; a law against speaking ill of the dead; restrictions on the clothing to be worn by women in public and on the exhibition of grief at funerals; differential fines for rapists; exact directions for tree planting; and the prescription of the length of wooden collars for fierce dogs. Since Solon was regarded as *the* Wise Man and Lawgiver of Athens, his memory attracted rather indiscriminately ideas or ordinances regarded as belonging to antiquity. Consequently it is difficult to form a pattern of his policies on the basis of the folklore about him, especially on the basis of selective quotations.

A remarkable note is struck by Plutarch's reference to the actual *axon*, or wooden tablet, on which a cited law was written: he claimed that fragments of the original tablets were still preserved in Athens in his day. In two other cases also (an amnesty law, and one regulating the prices of sacrificial victims) Plutarch cites the relevant tablet. From this we might conclude that, even if Plutarch did not himself consult the fragments, the tablets should have been available for consultation by fourth-century scholars, and were in fact consulted; otherwise how would they know the number of the tablet? The authenticity of the quoted laws seems at first sight assured: but grounds for doubt remain. The amnesty law seems, both in language and content, incompatible with a Solonian origin,[1] and Plutarch himself is forced to suppose that there may be some confusion or omission in its form: in the case of the sacrificial victims law, Plutarch also expresses surprise at the discrepancy in the level of prices given. The law banning exports except oil, explained as an attempt to conserve food supplies in Attica, would hardly have been compatible with any encouragement of trade, and the point of banning Athens' main (?) export, wine, is obscure. Even if we suppose the law to have been authentic, we must concede that it was unworkable. At any rate the archaeological record shows no trace of its effect; as far as we know, wine exports actually expanded during the sixth century. When Plutarch cites the number of the tablet, he is quoting from a source unknown to us, and on whose reliability we cannot pass an opinion. We may however surmise that the citations are from a code of laws available at Athens before the official revision began in 410 BC. Although this code was itself the result of revisions and additions since the time of Solon, in popular parlance it was still regarded as (substantially) Solonian, and even after the fifth-century revision people still continued so to regard it. As an authority for this we have as witness none other than Cicero, himself

---

[1] For a discussion of the authenticity of the *axones* see *HAC*, 22–7; Ruschenbusch, *Solonos Nomoi, Historia Einzelschriften* 9; R. S. Stroud, *The Axones and Kurbeis of Drakon and Solon*, University of California Publications in Classical Studies 19, 1979.

a lawyer and a scholar steeped in Greek history and literature, who stated (*Pro Roscio Amerino* 70) that in his own day the *Athenians were still living under the laws of Solon.*

VIII CHANGES TO THE LAWS AND THE INSTITUTIONS

Aristotle's book is concerned with the evolution of the Athenian constitution which, in his view, passed through eleven stages until it reached its completed form (its 'fulfilment') in the fourth-century democracy. According to his reckoning it reached, with Solon, its third stage, which provided the basis for the later democratic constitution, and to that extent it could be claimed that Solon was the founder of the democracy, in opposition to the view commonly held in the fifth century, that the founder of Athenian democracy had been Cleisthenes. At the beginning of Aristotle's exposition of Solon's constitutional arrangements, a distinction is made between this work and the 'other laws' of Solon; hence the references to the laws on homicide, which were not changed by Solon, and the earlier lawgiver, Dracon, whose historicity was assumed by fourth-century writers: a surviving inscription, unfortunately in very poor condition, purports to quote from a copy of one of Dracon's laws. According to Athenian tradition, Solon was not the first to frame a code of written law for Athens.

(a) Solon established a constitution, together with other laws: henceforth [the Athenians] dispensed with the laws made by Dracon, except for those concerning homicide. The [new] laws were inscribed on the tablets (*kurbeis*, and set up in the Royal Portico:[1] everyone promised on oath to observe them. . . . Solon made the laws binding for one hundred years.[2]

The following are the constitutional arrangements which he made. On the basis of an assessment [of wealth] he made a division into four groups, as they had previously been divided. The groups were: *pentakosiomedimnoi* (five-hundred-measure men); *hippeis* (cavaliers); *zeugitae* (teamsters); and *thetes* (labourers). To the first three groups he assigned the major offices, that is, the nine archons, the stewards, the sellers, the eleven, and the treasurers, offices being assigned to each group on the basis of its assessment. To members of the labourers' group he conceded only the right of participation in the public assembly, and in the law courts.[3] To qualify as a 'five-hundred-measure man' one had to produce five hundred measures, dry and liquid combined, from one's own property; as a 'cavalier' three hundred. (Others claim that the qualification in this case was the capability of maintaining a horse, on the grounds that the name of the group was derived from its function, and also citing the votive offerings of olden times . . . but it is more logical that their qualification should have been reckoned by the measure of their produce, just like the 'five-hundred-measure men'.) The teamsters comprised those producing two hundred measures combined. The rest were in the labourers' group, and had no participation in office-bearing. So it is that even today, when a candidate about to draw lots for an office is asked to state his rating, he would never say that it was of the labourers' group.

Solon instituted the procedure of filling the offices of state by drawing lots from candidates pre-selected by each tribe, each pre-selecting ten candidates for the nine archons, who were then balloted from this short list.[4] Hence the surviving custom for the tribes each to ballot ten, then to draw lots. Proof that Solon had offices filled by lot in accordance with the assessment arrangements is the law on the appointment of treasurers which is still in force today: it prescribes that treasurers be balloted from the *pentakosiomedimnoi*. Such were the procedures for the appointment of the nine archons, as Solon instituted them by law. In the old days it was the Areopagus Council that would summon, and decide on its own responsibility, the most suitable candidate for each of the public offices, and appoint him to act for the following year. There were to be four *tribes*, as before, and four *tribe kings*. Each of the tribes was divided into three *trittyes* and twelve *naucraries*. In charge of the latter were officials termed *naucrari*, who had responsibility for raising the levies and expending them. Hence, in the laws of Solon which are no longer in force, there often occur the phrases 'the naucrari are to exact . . .', and 'to draw upon the naucrary account'.[5]

Solon also instituted a Council of Four Hundred, one hundred from each tribe:[6] and he appointed the Council of the Areopagus to be watchdog over the laws, in accordance with its traditional function of safeguarding the political arrangements. This body controlled most of the important affairs of state, and called before it wrongdoers, with authority to impose fines and other penalties. It deposited on the Acropolis the money exacted, without recording the grounds for the penalty. It also sat in judgement upon those attempting to subvert the people's authority:[7] against such offenders Solon had brought in a law of impeachment. And because he observed that the city was often in a state of conflict (*stasis*) but some of the citizens were, through apathy, inclined to let things take their course, he introduced a law specifically directed at them, directing that, at a time of civic strife, anyone who failed to bear arms on either side should lose his citizen rights and be excluded from the life of the state.[8]

Aristotle, AP 7–8

(b) Solon established the Council of the Areopagus, composed of men who had held the annual office of archon: as an ex-archon himself, he was a member of the council. He saw that the people were still restive and aggressive after their release from debts, so he formed a second council, choosing one hundred men from each of the four tribes. He directed that this body should consider in advance all business before it was presented to a public assembly, and not permit anything to be brought forward there which had not been so discussed. Thus he set up the council [of the Areopagus] as an overall supervisor over the whole corporation, and as a guardian of the constitution, thinking that the state, moored by two councils like two anchors, would be less storm-tossed, and would keep the populace more in a state of equilibrium.

Plutarch, Solon 19

---

1. See Section VII(c) for reference to the *axones* or *kurbeis*, the wooden tablets on which Solon's laws are said to have been inscribed. There is no doubt that, in the fifth century, there was in existence a written code of laws which was claimed to be a copy of those made by Solon. The difficult question to answer is, how strong were the grounds for ascribing them to Solon? It would immensely improve the credibility of Aristotle's narrative if we could believe that it was based on the scrutiny, even at second or third hand, of an accurate copy of the code. For in none of the quotations from Solon's poems, which are Aristotle's only known authentic source, is there any reference to constitutional law. Unfortunately it is hard to believe that the Solonian code, as the fifth century knew it, was genuine. Trust in its authenticity must rest on the belief that the original wooden tablets had survived intact for nearly two hundred years, which had included the Persian occupation of Athens and the sack of the Acropolis; or else that an accurate copy had been made from the original tablets, and had been kept in its original form, in spite of all the subsequent changes and additions. Trust in the fifth-century copy cannot but be adversely affected by the apparent carelessness with which Athenian writers and speakers attributed any ancient enactments to Solon; and it may be significant that in discussing the authenticity of any particular measure, argument seemed always to be conducted on the grounds of probability (as in the case of Androtion's theory) rather than by reference to a copy of the law in question.

2. The term of one hundred years is echoed by Plutarch (*Solon* 25), but contradicted

by Herodotus (1.29), who gives ten years as the time of trial (see Section III). If it was indeed ever contemplated that the legal system of the state would resist change for a century, the expectation was certainly to be disappointed.

3. Although Aristotle regarded Solon as an important figure in the development of the Athenian constitution, the sum of the achievements claimed for Solon in this field by Aristotle seem surprisingly unimpressive and vague. In chapters 3 and 4 of *AP* there is a brief sketch of what Aristotle believed to have been the institutional arrangements at Athens in pre-Solonian times: we ought to be able to estimate the contribution to reform made by Solon (or rather, the contribution claimed by Aristotle for Solon) by a comparison of the reforms mentioned in chapters 7–9 with the earlier arrangements mentioned in chapters 3 and 4.

In the latter it is stated that appointment to the highest office of state, the archonship, had earlier been on the basis of 'birth and wealth'. At a later stage, in the constitution brought in by Dracon, political control was vested in the class of those who bore arms (the hoplites) who chose the archons and the stewards from a group owning assets worth at least 10 minas; the other magistrates were appointed by, and from, the hoplites themselves; the *strategoi* (army commanders) and the *hipparchoi* (cavalry commanders) were appointed from a group owning assets of at least 100 minas. The Council of the Areopagus 'guarded the laws' and judged offenders, 'as before'. There was a council of 401 members chosen by lot from the body of full citizens (= the hoplites?).

It would appear therefore that Solon replaced the ancient criteria of 'birth and wealth' for high office by the criterion of (rural) wealth, plus the ability to bear arms, which included the means to provide them, so that the hoplite qualification was also to some extent a criterion of wealth. It has therefore been claimed by modern historians that an achievement of Solon was to replace birth by wealth, as the basis for political leadership in Athens. The term 'birth' is a vague one, but we hear (in *AP* 13 and elsewhere) of an aristocratic Athenian caste, the *Eupatrids* (men of high degree), who were regarded as the traditional ruling group in early times. The reference to 'birth' as a political criterion may therefore be taken as a reference to the role of the Eupatrids and their early monopoly of political leadership at Athens. Thus, it is suggested, the real force of Solon's reform was not so much to change the *machinery* of government as to change the basis of political *leadership*, and this had the effect of opening its ranks to men who had hitherto been excluded by reason of birth or rank. The property classes recognized by Solon, or devised by him, were defined solely in terms of farm produce – cereals, wine and oil – not in money terms. The 'new men' admitted to the governing class by Solon's reform would therefore have to be wealthy landowners – perhaps minor aristocracy, or men from areas of Attica other than the plain of Athens which was traditionally the stronghold of the Eupatrids. The reported change lends no support for any suggestion that a purpose was to open the doors of political leadership to a non-landed class of wealthy merchants or entrepreneurs, even if such existed as an identifiable group in Solonian Athens.

It would be possible to challenge this view on the grounds that, in chapter 4 of *AP*, eligibility for office in pre-Solonian times is expressed in money terms, which implies that Athens was operating a money-based economy in the seventh century BC (when coinage had scarcely begun in Greece). This, however, is not the only feature of Aristotle's account in chapter 4 that inspires scepticism. In particular there is a startling difference in the assessments necessary to qualify for the offices of archon and *strategos*, the latter assessment being ten times higher than the former for what was traditionally the highest office of state. The relative status of the two offices is quite anachronistic as applied to the early period; it is, however, a reasonably accurate estimate of their relative status in the later fifth century. Secondly, the idea of political power resting exclusively in the hands of the hoplite class (i.e. only they would have voting rights) sounds like a quotation taken from the proposals for reform in Athens in 411 BC, a time when, it is suspected, the 'constitution of Dracon' was invented as part of a political platform. Such suspicions have undermined the credibility of Aristotle's sketch in chapter 4, and made very much harder the task of deciding the extent of constitutional change effected by Solon.

4. The statement that the final choice of the archons was made by drawing lots has been doubted on two main grounds. In the first place the statement seems to be contradicted by Aristotle in *Politics* (see Section IX(d) below). Secondly, there seems to be an inherent improbability in the idea of allowing the man whose responsibility it was to lead the armed forces to be chosen in this random way. The use of lot for filling posts of lesser responsibility was regarded as a typical practice of an advanced democracy; it is to be noted that even in its later, most radical form, democratic Athens did not choose its generals by lot. On the other hand, to reject a statement in a source merely on grounds of plausibility, in an area about which we know so little, is itself rather dangerous.

5. In his account of Cylon's unsuccessful coup Herodotus referred to the 'presidents of the naucraries' as the chief magistrates of Athens at the time (see Section I(a)), a statement denied by Thucydides. There are scattered references elsewhere to the naucraries as small districts, and the naucrari as the head men of such districts; such men were later termed *demarchs*. To Aristotle naucraries were evidently subdivisions of the citizen body, and their heads were charged with some financial responsibilities. He was perhaps relying for this information mainly on the quotations he gives from the 'obsolete laws of Solon'; as we do not know the source of the quotations (and we can hardly suppose that Aristotle had himself seen these 'obsolete laws') it is hard to form any idea of their value as evidence. The form of the word naucrary would naturally suggest a connection with ships (*naukleros* = ship's master), and etymology may be responsible for many of the theories about the naucraries. If they were, as has been suggested, connected with the financing of state shipping (assuming that the early Attic state possessed any ships), it would be reasonable to explain their complete disappearance from the scene later on the grounds that their functions disappeared for good when the organization (or reorganization) of Athenian state fighting ships took place in 483 BC.

6. As Aristotle does not indicate what were intended to be the functions of this new council, we may conclude that he assumed them to be similar to the functions of the Council of Five Hundred in his own day; and this is what Plutarch also assumed. Doubts have been expressed about the existence of this Council of Four Hundred; first, because it seems like an anachronism, and secondly because of a suspicious resemblance to the 'Council of Four Hundred' which the oligarchic

reformers ordained in 411 BC, claiming that they were returning to the 'ancestral constitution' (a constitution which, it is suspected, never existed outside fifth-century political propaganda). The need for such a council as Solon is said to have introduced arises from the principle that all public business must be scrutinized and debated by a people's council, acting as a steering committee, before such business can be submitted to the assembly. This principle was a basic and distinctive feature of the later advanced democracy at Athens; but it seems stangely misplaced at this early stage of the evolution of the democratic constitution. It is not, perhaps, an important argument that we have no record of any action by this council, for the detailed knowledge we possess is, after all, very meagre indeed. What seems anachronistic is the assumption underlying the need for such a council, that the volume of business likely to come before the assembly at that stage would require a steering committee of that kind. One cannot help noting the apparent incongruity of the tradition with the belief that the laws were to remain unchanged for at least ten years. It must, however, be borne in mind that lack of supporting evidence and apparent improbability are not in themselves adequate to disprove an explicit statement by Aristotle, and many scholars accept the existence of such a council. They can point to the fact that such a popular council did indeed exist about 600 BC on the island of Chios, if the epigraphists are right in so dating an inscription found on the island, referring to a 'popular council'.

7. Aristotle's statement that Solon appointed the Areopagus Council to perform its traditional functions seems to mean that, in his view, Solon made no change to its powers or functions, and in fact his statement in chapter 8 echoes almost word for word his earlier summary, in chapter 3, of the functions of the council in archaic times. In his biography of Solon Plutarch retailed another tradition (see (b) above), that Solon had himself inaugurated the Areopagus Council.

8. Such a law seems highly improbable, as Plutarch (*Solon* 20) remarked, but not, apparently, to Aristotle; and we may simply choose to believe, or disbelieve, him. Evidence against the existence of any such law has, however, been offered by Hignett (*HAC*, 27). In the late fifth century a defendant, charged with absenting himself from Athens during the civil war of 404–403 BC, argued that he was guilty of no crime, as there was no law against such conduct. Instead of referring to the alleged law of Solon, the prosecutor, Lysias, declared that the crime was so monstrous that *no lawgiver would have thought of legislating against it*. We can safely say that if such a law of Solon existed, Lysias had never heard of it.

IX   SOME VIEWS ON SOLON'S ACHIEVEMENT

(a) To the demos I gave such privilege as is fitting,
    neither diminishing it, nor offering more:
    those that held power, and were graced with wealth,
    I saw that they too suffered no indignity.

I stood, protecting both with my strong shield,
and allowed neither side to prevail in unjust victory.

Aristotle, AP 12.1

(b) I wrote down laws binding upon base and noble alike,
devising unswerving justice for each and every man.
Another who held the whip hand, as I did,
one of evil mind and full of greed,
would not have kept in check the populace.
For had I chosen the way that enemies wished,
or, again, what others planned for *them*,
this city would have been bereft of many men.
And so, I stood, on guard on every side,
twisting like a wolf amid a pack of hounds.

AP 12.4

(c) The following appear to be the three most democratic features of Solon's legislation:[1] first and most important, the prohibition of loans on personal security; secondly, the right of anyone to seek redress on behalf of victims of injustice; and thirdly, the thing which men say contributed more than anything else to the power of the masses, the right of appeal to a jury-court. For when the people are masters of the courts, they are masters of the state.

AP 9

(d) Some consider Solon to have been important as a lawgiver, for he put an end to a far too narrowly based government; liberated from servitude the common man; and established our traditional style of democracy, skilfully blending the governmental arrangements. I mean that the Council of the Areopagus was the oligarchic element in it; the elective offices[2] were the aristocratic element; and the jury-courts were the popular element. Certain institutions already in existence, for example the Council and the election of the magistrates, Solon seems merely to have left alone, but he seems really to have brought the demos into existence by constituting the jury-courts from the whole citizenry. And it is for this that some blame him, for removing alternative [organs], while making the court, chosen by lot, all-powerful. As it gained in strength, men courted its favour as if it were a tyrant, and so brought into being the present people's democracy. . . . Solon, it is true, seems to have given into the hands of the people only the minimal essentials of power, that is the right to elect[3] the magistrates and call them to account; and if it lacked this right the demos would be nothing more than a slave and an enemy alien. But he reserved all the offices for the upper class and the wealthy, the *pentakosiomedimnoi*, the *zeugitae*, and the third property class known as the *cavaliers*; but the fourth class, the *thetes*, was ineligible for any office.

Aristotle, *Politics* 1273b 36–1274a 22

---

1. It is surprising to find, in Aristotle's estimate of 'the most democratic features' of Solon's work, no reference to any change in the machinery of government, for example to the institution of the Council of Four Hundred, which one tradition assigned to him. All three measures mentioned by Aristotle are concerned primarily not with government but with civil rights. In *Politics* Aristotle gives Solon general credit for establishing the style of democratic government, but also stresses the 'liberation' aspect of Solon's achievement. The jury courts, attributed to Solon, were thought not only to have established protection for the rights of the common citizen, but also to have guaranteed to the latter some measure of control over the conduct of the high magistrates; the right to call them to account meant that the people, in the last resort, controlled how government machinery worked. It appears that the fourth-century historians could find in Solon's poetry only the vaguest idea of what changes he claimed to have made to the constitution: his expressed claims extend only to a general statement of fair dealing for all in his laws, and a belief that he has, by mediation, saved bloodshed. Faced with this element of uncertainty, Aristotle chooses to stress the humanitarian aspect, emphasized by Solon himself, and reasons that, by a reform to the system of common justice, Solon not only protected his people against wrong but also put into their hands the ultimate control over policy, by the right to call to account the elected magistrates. Solon, according to Aristotle, was no radical, as is seen by his reservation of all important offices for the wealthy; but his humanitarian concern for protecting the rights of the weak led finally to the demos virtually taking over the state.
2. & 3. Note the contradiction with *AP* 8 (Section VIII n.4).

X   STRIFE IN ATHENS

So, for these reasons, Solon went abroad;[1] and after his departure from the scene the city remained in a state of conflict. For four years they kept the peace, but in the fifth year after Solon's archonship conflict prevented the appointment of any archon;[2] four years later no archons were appointed, for the same reason. Then, after another four years, Damasias was chosen as archon, and held on to office for two years and two months, until he was forcibly driven out of office. Then, because of the continuing conflict, they [the Athenians] decided to choose ten archons, five from the *Eupatrids*, three from the *agroikoi*, and two from the *demiourgoi*:[3] these held the archonship during the year after Damasias. This proves that it was the archon who wielded the greatest power [at the time]; for this was the office that was apparently the main bone of contention.

Aristotle AP 13.1–2

1. On the alleged reasons for Solon's absence from Athens see Section III.
2. A comment in Plato (*Hippias Major* 285e) implies that there was available in the fourth century what was believed to be an authentic list of chief archons (by whose names the years were dated in the official record) going back to Solon. The date of his archonship is given by Diogenes Laertius (1.62) as two years after the 46th Olympiad, that is 594–593 BC. This date is generally accepted by modern historians. (Those who suggest a later date for Solon's reforms believe that they may have been carried out some time after his archonship, when he was appointed to a special office as mediator in the conflict.) It is therefore believed that the years of official 'anarchy' when no archons were appointed (or, conversely, their appointments were at some later stage declared illegal and struck from the record) were 590–589, and 586–585; and that Damasias' archonship began in 582–581 and was prolonged into the year 580 BC. One notes the plausibility of dating the reforms of Solon, and his extraordinary appointment, *after* the years of crisis, described in this chapter, rather than before them.
3. The Eupatrids (see Section VIII(a) n.4) were the traditional ruling élite whose homes and sphere of influence were in the central plain of Attica, on which stood the city of Athens. The other two terms, *agroikoi* (farmers, or ruralists), and *demiourgoi* (craftsmen, or public workers), were social groupings in myth about early Attica: the terms are not elsewhere used with reference to official classes or groupings. In myth the farmers and workers made up the commons – later to be termed the demos – in distinction from the nobles. Thus the coalition was believed to be a power-sharing temporary arrangement between nobles and non-nobles. The story could not have been derived from the archon list: its source lies in folklore, and it would be hazardous to rely upon its authenticity.
   See L. Gernet, 'Les dix archontes de 581', *Rev. Phil.* 12, 1948, 225 ff.

XI   THE GROWTH OF TYRANNY

As Greece became stronger, and made unprecedented progress in the acquisition of wealth, tyrannies took over fairly generally in the cities, as revenues increased. (The ancient form of government had been hereditary monarchies based on fixed privileges.) Greece at this time began to fit out

fleets, and the sea element became a greater centre of attention than before.
Thucydides 1.13

The note comes from Thucydides' Introduction to his *History of the Peloponnesian War*, in a survey of the growth of seapower in Greece, which he related to economic progress in the city-states. As a consequence of these two factors, or, at least, in combination with them, came a series of changes to the internal government of the cities, with the appearance of new, autocratic forms of government. The epoch to which he refers is that of archaic Greece, before the time of recorded history: he gives a dating by reference to a great sea battle between Corinth and Corcyra, its colony, about 650 BC, and to Polycrates of Samos, who lived in the time of the Persian king Cambyses, who conquered Egypt in 525 BC. Thucydides' theory thus implies that there was a logical and historical connection between the growth of maritime activity and the age of revolution in the seventh and sixth centuries BC.

Tyrannies appeared only in the *poleis*, the city-states, most of which were, at this early period, situated near the sea and were dependent, to a greater or lesser extent, upon maritime trade and communications. The growth of seapower, the emergence of the *polis* as a characteristic community structure, economic growth, revolution in the cities, and the arrival of the tyranny in Greece, together form a simplified, but illuminating, theory of historical progress. Unfortunately the history of other early tyrannies is known only in minor details; the only one of which a considerable body of legend survives is that of sixth-century Athens.

XII   THE FACTIONS IN ATTICA

(a) The Athenians of the Shore and those of the Plain were locked in conflict, the former led by Megacles, the son of Alcmaeon, the men of the Plain led by Lycurgus, son of Aristolaides. Peisistratus, with an eye to setting up a tyranny, collected a third group. He formed a group of partisans, and, posing as a champion of the men from beyond the hills,[1] he devised the following ruse. He inflicted wounds on himself and his mules, then drove his carriage into the agora, pretending that he had just escaped from enemies, who were supposed to have tried to assassinate him as he was driving into the country. He begged the demos to provide him with a bodyguard. (Previously he had won distinction in the command of troops against the Megarians, when he had captured Nisaea, and had achieved other notable successes.[2]) The Athenian demos was quite deceived, and acceded to his request, assigning to him a band of citizens – not spearmen, but club bearers – who were to accompany him, armed with wooden clubs. These men followed Peisistratus in an insurrection which seized the Acropolis. That was how Peisistratus began to rule Athens; though he did not interfere with the existing offices, nor did he change the official ordinances, but he ran the state according to the established forms, in a fine and efficient style of government.

Herodotus 1.59

(b) In their internal affairs the Athenians continued to be a sick society. Some saw the source, and the reason, for their problems in the cancellation of debts, which had resulted in their own impoverishment; others resented the momentous change which had taken place in the political order; others again were motivated by personal feuds. There were three factions. One was that of the Shore people, whose leader was Megacles, son of Alcmaeon; their political stance was thought to be a middle-of-the-road style. Another was that of the Plain, whose aim was an oligarchy; their leader was Lycurgus. The third was that of the Hill, headed by Peisistratus, thought to be closest of all to the demos. Men drawn towards this faction included those impoverished by the debt cancellations, and those who felt threatened, as they were not of pure Athenian descent. (Evidence of this lies in the fact that after the fall of the tyranny there was a revision of the roll, on the ground that there were many registered as citizens who where not entitled to be so.) Each group owed its name to the areas where they had their farms.

Aristotle, AP 13

---

1. Herodotus' names for the three factions were followed by Aristotle in the *AP* (see above), except that whereas Herodotus terms Peisistratus' group as the 'men beyond the hills' (*Hyperakrioi*) Aristotle refers to them simply as the 'men of the hills' (*Diakrioi*). Herodotus' term is more specific, apparently referring to those dwelling (from the point of view of Athenian city people) beyond the range of Mount Hymettos, that is in the east and northeast of Attica. Apparently both writers are referring, in the terms used, to local areas of the country; they do not mean Plainsmen, Coasters, and Highlanders, in the sense of men living on flat, coastal, or hilly country anywhere in Attica, a concept which would make nonsense of the whole story. By the Plain is meant the central plain on which

stood the city of Athens. Thus the basic distinction between the three factions was thought to have been regional in character, as Aristotle says it was. In spite of this he had added to Herodotus' version a political interpretation of the factional conflict: the factions have become political parties of the Centre, the Right, and the Left. This should be understood as his own interpretation of the political aims and styles of the factional leaders; Plutarch, in his *Life of Solon* 29, also tried to fit the regional divisions into a political, or ideological, context. Neither made any serious attempt to explain how the regional divisions of sixth-century Attica could have fitted the political divisions of fourth-century Athens; social confrontation was assumed to be based in the end on the conflict between democrats and oligarchs. Some modern historians have also tried to reconcile the apparently regional nature of the strife with a clash of political or economic interests, but with little success. The explanation may be much simpler, lying in the personal feuds of nobles who lorded it over their own enclaves.

2. Nisaea was the port of Megara on its eastern coast; the conflict between Athens and Megara was of long standing, and concerned the possession of the offshore island of Salamis. Peisistratus is believed to have commanded as polemarch an Athenian task force against Megara. The tradition followed by Herodotus implies that it was his military background and reputation, rather than his local following, that enabled him to mount the force with which he seized power.

See P. N. Ure, *The Origin of Tyranny*, Cambridge 1922; A. French, 'Solon and the Megarian question', *JHS* 77, 1957; D. M. Lewis, 'Cleisthenes and Attica', *Historia* 12, 1963; R. J. Hopper, ' "Plain", "Shore", and "Hill" in early Athens', *ABSA* 56, 1961.

XIII   TYRANNY AT ATHENS

After his successful coup Peisistratus was apparently not able to control the situation for very long, and he was twice forced out of Athens by combinations of his enemies, the rival factions. During his second exile he travelled abroad, and laid the foundations for his second return, which was followed by thirty-six years of rule.[1]

(a) Peisistratus . . . left the country altogether, and went to Eretria.[2] There he discussed the position with his sons: the view of Hippias was that a further attempt be made to regain the tyranny; and this was the view that prevailed. They proceeded to collect contributions from such cities as were under some kind of obligation to them. They received large sums from a number of cities, but the richest source of funds came from Thebes. There was some lapse of time, and then all was made ready for the return. Argive mercenary soldiers arrived from the Peloponnesus; and a man of Naxos, named Lygdamis, volunteered his support; he brought money and men with him, and also boundless enthusiasm.[3] In the eleventh year of their exile they sailed from Eretria for home, and made their first landfall in Attica at Marathon. As they were encamped at this place they were joined by their supporters from the town, and others, for whom tyranny was preferable to freedom, streamed in from the villages: thus the whole force was assembled. While Peisistratus had been collecting supplies, and, later, when he held Marathon, the Athenians in the town had not taken the matter seriously. But when they learned that he was moving from Marathon on to the town, at that point they took the field against him. Thus they marched in full force to confront the returning exiles, while Peisistratus' men, on their way from Marathon towards the city, met them near a temple of Athena at Pallene. The two armies faced each other. It was at that point that a prophet, Amphilytos of Acarnania, was inspired to accost Peisistratus, and standing before him, he spoke a verse:

> Cast is the net, and the mesh is spread:
> the fishes will come swarming through the moonlit night.

Thus spoke the prophet, and Peisistratus, understanding the prophecy, declared his acceptance of it, and gave the order to advance.[4] At that time the Athenians from the town were intent on their meal, followed by dicing, or the siesta. Thus Peisistratus' troops fell upon them, and routed them. . . . For the third time he made himself master of Athens. He established his tyranny on a firm basis, with the aid of a large force of hired troops and of revenues, some from Attica, others from around the river Strymon.[5] He took as hostages the sons of those Athenians who had remained, and had not immediately fled, depositing them at the island of Naxos, which he had captured by force and had put under the control of Lygdamis. In addition, he 'purified' the island of Delos[6] . . . Thus he ruled Athens as tyrant. Some of the Athenians had fallen in battle; others left their homes and went into exile with the Alcmaeonids.

Herodotus 1.61–4

(b) Peisistratus was driven out of the country for the second time about six years after his [first] return: he had not lasted very long. Because of his decision not to consummate his marriage with Megacles' daughter he grew afraid of the other two factions, and withdrew.[7] One of his first moves was to take part in a colonial venture at a place called Rhaecelus, on the gulf of Thermae. From there he moved to the vicinity of Mount Pangaeum, where he gained riches, and hired soldiers.[8] Ten years later he returned to Eretria, and only then did he attempt to restore his regime by force. In this he had the assistance of a number of allies, in particular certain Thebans, Lygdamis of Naxos, and also the Cavaliers of Eretria, who were in political control of that place. Peisistratus won the battle of Pallene, captured the city of Athens, and confiscated the arms of the commoners; this time he took vigorous measures to maintain his regime. After capturing Naxos, he appointed Lygdamis to rule it.

Aristotle, *AP* 15.1–3

---

1. Peisistratus' first seizure of power is dated to 561–560; the tyranny came finally to an end in 510, when his son Hippias was expelled from Athens. Herodotus claimed (5.65) that they (the Peisistratids) had then ruled for thirty-six years. If this means, as is usually assumed, that the ruling house had been in uninterrupted control for that period, then the final return to power of Peisistratus must have been in 546–545. These figures are generally accepted by historians. But the chronology of the exiles is a total muddle; the figures given by Aristotle in *AP* can hardly be right, as they would bring back Peisistratus to Athens for his third, and longest, period of power only a year before he is said to have died. Aristotle's figures are also irreconcilable with the set of figures supplied by Herodotus, and at one point are contradicted by Aristotle in *Politics* (1315b 31–4). We may accept as comparatively firm the dates 560 for the first coup, 546 for the final return of Peisistratus, and 510 for the end of the dynasty. For a discussion of the intermediate dates, see T. J. Cadoux, *JHS* 68, 1949, 104–9; Moore, *Aristotle and Xenophon on Democracy and Oligarchy*, 229–30; J. G. F. Hind, 'The tyrannies and the exiles of Pisistratos', *Classical Quarterly* 24, 1974, 14–17; P. J. Rhodes, 'Pisistratid chronology again', *Phoenix* 30, 1976, 195–6.
2. Eretria was about twenty miles from Athens, on the west coast of the island of Euboea.
3. Peisistratus, like other exiles, dropped out of sight while abroad, so that the usual gossip and folklore, which became the raw material for history, is missing for those periods. How such men survived, and even managed to return richer than they left, is a matter of conjecture. Herodotus gives one suggestion: they were supported by their fellow nobles in other cities with whom their families had personal ties, perhaps dynastic, and also formal ties of guest friendship. But the actions abroad of Peisistratus, and others of his type, do not suggest that they were content merely to live as pensioners at an alien court. The one profession for which they were qualified was that of leadership, especially in war: the seventh and sixth centuries saw the development of a new kind of professional soldier, well armed and trained to fight in formation, the hoplites. The tyrannies which were established at Corinth, at Sicyon and at Athens were all the result of an armed coup by leaders at the head of trained soldiers. We may therefore guess that Peisistratus made use abroad of his military experience, and took service abroad (as Miltiades was later to do, when he fought as part of a Persian task force). Peisistratus returned to Athens at the head of a band of professional soldiers: it was perhaps as a captain of mercenaries that he, and Lygdamis, had lived.

But mercenaries, unlike local conscripts, have to be paid, if they are to be kept together for long. The source of funds can be pillage. Perhaps here is one connection which Thucydides saw between maritime development and tyranny: where trade flourished, so did piracy, both on sea and on land. Another source of enrichment was in foreign service, or the kind of colonial venture mentioned by Aristotle in (b) above. Adventurers like Peisistratus of Athens, or Polycrates of Samos, needed money to pay soldiers, and soldiers to sustain their following. Tyranny arrived when they used their troops no longer in raiding and extortion, but in a frontal assault on the centre of control in their own land.

4. The anecdote illustrates one aspect of Herodotus' *History* which might be overlooked in a collection of extracts selected for their value as historical source material. An accomplished historian, Herodotus was also a creative writer and a teller of strange tales in the fashion of old epic, stories in which prophecy, predestination, and the working of a divine purpose are almost as common as in the poems of Solon. The sense of tragic mystery which pervades Herodotus' wide canvas contrasts with the earnest rationalism of the scholarly Aristotle.

5. See (b) n.8 below.

6. The small island of Delos was regarded as the religious centre of the Ionian people, and they regularly gathered there from many centres, including Athens, for festivals in honour of Apollo. The symbolic purification was carried out by the removal of graves from a part of the sacred island. The job was completed by Athens during the Peloponnesian War, allegedly as an act of thanksgiving for the ending of the plague. In both cases the pious, and publicized, action was perhaps intended to advertise that the centre of Ionian tradition was now under the protection and patronage of Athens. One may suppose that it was the later purification that recalled into the arena of recorded history the earlier action by Peisistratus, which was also mentioned by Thucydides (3.104).

7. Aristotle's account is taken from that in Herodotus. Peisistratus was driven into exile by a combination of his two rival factions; but their leaders subsequently quarrelled among themselves, and a new combination between the Alcmaeonid-led faction (the Shore) and the Peisistratid faction secured his return. The deal was sealed by a dynastic marriage between Peisistratus and the daughter of the Alcmaeonid Megacles. (The scene of the homecoming was spectacular, with the tyrant escorted home personally by a 'goddess', a pretty local girl dressed in armour to look like Athena. Aristotle, rather surprisingly, carried the story, while describing the trick as 'simplistic' and naming Herodotus as his source; the latter had gone further, and described it as one of the silliest tricks he had ever come across!) After this encouraging, if symbolic, union with a goddess, it seems not surprising that the actual dynastic marriage ran on to the rocks, leaving Peisistratus out in the cold.

8. 'The rapid development of trade between the Thraco-Macedonian area and the Aegean and Asia drew the attention of Greek adventurers. Peisistratus of Athens formed a settlement on the high table-land, called Rhaecalus, which overlooks the plain of Sednes, when he was driven out of Athens c. 555. Here on a promontory jutting into the Thermaic Gulf he was well placed to engage in or interfere with trade. Later he moved to the region of Mt. Pangaeum, where he made money and hired soldiers for the *coup d'état* at Athens in 546. During these years the Thracians were the leading people in these areas, and he evidently

collaborated with them. In both places he was attracted, we may assume, by the trade in gold and silver. At Rhaecalus he may have anticipated the role of Aenea, his immediate neighbour, as an intermediary in this trade.'
N. G. L. Hammond, *History of Macedonia*, vol. II, Oxford 1979, 68.

XIV PEISISTRATUS AS RULER

Aristotle follows his main source, Herodotus (see Section XII(a)) in his positive attitude to Peisistratus as tyrant; the same view is expressed by Thucydides (see XVI(b) below). It is at first sight astonishing that the autocratic rule of this noble usurper became regarded as a positive step towards democracy, and one notes that the good press accorded to his rule contrasts with the very bad press generally accorded by contemporary Greek writers to the fifth-century Athenian democracy. On the other hand Athenian tradition hailed the eventual fall of the tyranny as a liberation: these two apparently contradictory views are reconciled by the belief that when power passed to Peisistratus' successor(s), the character of the regime changed. It would appear that the objection was not to autocracy as such, but only to the misuse of its power.

This was how Peisistratus' rule was originally established, and such were its vicissitudes. As I have said, his administration of Athens was one of moderation, and he acted more like a citizen than an autocrat.[1] In general, he was humane, easy-going, and forgiving to wrongdoers; in particular, he advanced money to those in difficulties, to maintain them at work, so that they could continue in subsistence farming. In this he had two motives: first, so that they should not spend their time in the city, but remain scattered over the countryside; and secondly, so that, living in modest affluence, their attention should remain concentrated on their private lives, and they should have neither the will nor the time for politics.[2] At the same time the cultivation of the land meant an increase in his revenues: for he levied a tax of 10 per cent on the produce of the land.[3] This was also the reason why he organized local courts in the villages; he frequently made personal tours of inspection to the country, settling disputes, so that people should not come to town and neglect their work.

There is a story that on one of Peisistratus' visits there occurred the incident of the man cultivating, on Mount Hymettos, what subsequently came to be known as the 'tax-free block of land'. Peisistratus caught sight of a man industriously digging at what was nothing but stones. Much surprised, he bade his servant enquire of the man what he was growing there. 'Nothing but aches and pains', said the man, ' and of these aches and pains a tithe goes to Peisistratus'. The man had replied without knowing who he was talking to, but Peisistratus was gratified by his openness and his industry, and absolved him from any tax.

In other regards too, the rule of Peisistratus was not oppressive: peace and quiet was his constant aim. So it was commonly said that the tyranny of Peisistratus was a Golden Age, for later on, when his sons took over, the regime became much harsher. The greatest tribute paid to him was for his democratic approach and friendly style. He was in general anxious to conduct administration according to the law,[4] without giving himself any advantage, and in particular, on one occasion when he was summoned to the court of the Areopagus to answer a charge of murder, he turned up in person to present his case. His accuser however withdrew in fright. It was for this reason that he stayed so long in power; and when he was driven out, he easily regained his position. Most of the gentry and the commoners supported him: the former were won over by his social graces, the latter by the practical help he gave them in their private concerns. He had an admirable approach to both of them. At that time the Athenians' laws about tyrants were mild, in particular the law concerning the imposition of a tyranny. The law was as follows: 'Herewith the decrees and the traditional rules; if there be any insurrection leading to a tyranny, or anyone assist in the same, let him be outlawed, and his issue after him'.

Aristotle, AP 16

---

1. Attitudes to tyranny in the fifth century, when Herodotus wrote, were coloured by the fact that Greek tyrants had actively collaborated with the Persian invaders and governed in their name (Hippias provided a particularly bad example of such collaboration). In Herodotus' *History*, the narrative of the Persian war is set within a metaphysical pattern of human endeavour which reaches beyond the natural and permitted limits (symbolized in the crossing of a natural frontier), and overreaches itself in the infatuation of power, the trap which entices, then destroys its victim. The fatal attraction of power is shown not only in the external clash, but also in the internal social divisions: the defeat of the Persians and their Greek collaborators asserts the freedom of the Greeks externally, but also internally, by their rejection of tyranny. In treating other Greek tyrants, Cypselus, Thrasybulus and Polycrates, Herodotus shows the doomed sequence of violence, success, magnificence, infatuation, and ruin. But Peisistratus breaks the pattern; he shuns violence, despotism, and self-destruction. To carry the tradition further, Plato in the *Republic* (560) puts forward the sequence of democracy > permissive chaos > tyranny; whereas the sequence appears in the Athenian tradition as chaos > tyranny > democracy.

2. In *Politics* 1313a Aristotle discusses the methods used by tyrannies to preserve themselves, both by repression and precautions, and also by conciliation. The former category includes not only the liquidation of suspects, the prohibition of public or private meetings, the use of spies and provocateurs, but also devices to keep the subjects poor and busy, so they will have neither the time nor energy for plotting their own liberation; as one of the examples of the grandiose works undertaken as part of such a programme he quotes Peisistratus' temple of Olympian Zeus.

3. It would appear that Aristotle regarded the tax as primarily a device to keep the subjects poor; its value as revenue was a bonus. Thucydides (XVI(b) below) gives a different figure, 5 per cent, for the level of taxation. Why Aristotle contradicts him is not clear. How such a tax could have been calculated and collected is a mystery; it involves the difficult assumption that Peisistratus had at his disposal a network of bureaucracy. It is, on the other hand, entirely possible that food for Peisistratus' entourage was commissioned on a regular but informal basis from areas in easy reach of the city, and this could have been the origin of the belief. Aristotle's dependence on folklore is illustrated by his reference in the passage to two incidents which apparently originated in jokes, that of the ignorant labourer incautiously grumbling to the head of state without any idea to whom he was speaking, and that of that rash accuser who thought better of his complaint, and discreetly withdrew from the case. The point of the first joke, namely the impositions of the boss, could have been the origin of belief about the level of taxation, or even that such taxation was levied. Aristotle reasoned from his own principles of political economy that Peisistratus helped farmers, and then taxed them, in order to neutralize them politically; and Aristotle found material in the folklore to support such a theory. But it is possible that support for farming, decentralization of justice, and some sort of levy on production (assuming that the legend had foundation in reality) were designed for other ends, that is, a more efficient system of administration and economy, as many modern historians believe.

4. The view that the laws and the constitution functioned unchanged under the tyranny is hard to reconcile with the supposedly autocratic position of Peisistratus, and with Aristotle's own statement that 'the tyranny had consigned to oblivion the laws of Solon through their disuse' (*AP* 22.1).

For an illuminating discussion of the issues raised by this chapter see Day and Chambers, *Aristotle's History of Athenian Democracy*, 89–100.

XV EXTERNAL AFFAIRS

(a) Peisistratus took Sigeum by force from the Mytilenian settlers. After capturing it, he installed there as tyrant his own illegitimate son, Hegesistratus, whose mother was from Argos. Hegesistratus managed to hold on to all [the territory] that his father had given to him, but not without a struggle. Now there had been fighting for a long time between Mytilenians and Athenians, the former operating from the Achilleon settlement, the latter from Sigeum . . . among the events that had occurred in these engagements was one involving the poet Alcaeus. Once, when the Athenians were gaining the upper hand, he took to his heels and escaped. The Athenians however got hold of his weapons, and hung them up in Athena's temple in Sigeum. Alcaeus put the whole episode into a poem, relating his own discomfiture, and sent it to his friend Melanippus. The Mytilenians and Athenians had been reconciled by Cyselus' son, Periander, to whom they had committed the issue for arbitration; the terms were that both sides should remain in possession of what they held.

Herodotus 5.94–5

(b) Sigeum was occupied by Athenians: they had sent out Phrynon, the Olympic champion, though almost all of the Troad was claimed by the Lesbians . . . Pittacus of Mytilene, one of the so-called Seven Wise Men, sailed against the Athenian commander, Phrynon, and carried on operations against him that were as poor in conception as they were in results. This was when the poet Alcaeus, in his own words, was getting badly mauled in the battle, so he threw away his arms and fled . . . . The war continued for some time, until Periander was chosen by both sides as an arbitrator, and put an end to the conflict.

Strabo, *Geography* 13.1.38

Sigeum lies on the west coast of northern Asia Minor, southwest of Troy, south of the Hellespont and in reach of the straits. The 'City of Archilles' (Archilleon), settled from Mytilene, lay on the coast between Sigeum and the straits. Neither the Achilleon nor Sigeum were suitable bases from which to control the entrance to the straits, but were well situated to harass and plunder trading ships on this well-used route.

The passage in Herodotus is a flashback to explain how Athenians had come to be in possession of Sigeum in the first place. Peisistratus captured the place; but before that there had been a history of conflict, extending back to the seventh century. Phrynon, the Athenian commander, was believed to have won his Olympic event in 636–635 BC: Periander died in the first quarter of the sixth century. Events in this early war were immortalized by Alcaeus' poem, which would have been available to Aristotle, but is lost to us. Thus Peisistratus, in his adventure in the Troad, was following in the steps of much earlier Athenian adventurers. At a time when Solon was a boy, and (in the view of Aristotle) Attica was plunging into internal conflict and economic chaos, Athenian colonists were sailing abroad, to find a new home in the northeast. As Peisistratus had to recapture Sigeum, the earlier venture had evidently failed.

(c) Until now [493 BC] the ruler of this area [the Thracian Chersonese] had been Miltiades, the son of Cimon and grandson of Stesagoras. In earlier days the sovereignty over it had been won by Miltiades, son of Cypselus, in the following manner. This peninsula [the Chersonese] used to be occupied by the Dolonci, a Thracian tribe. When they were at war with the Apsinthians and things were going badly for them, they sent their head men to Delphi to consult the oracle about the war. The priestess of Apollo bade them bring in a new founder to their place; it should be the first man to offer them hospitality after they left the temple. The Dolonci then proceeded along the Sacred Way, passing through Phocis and Boeotia, and when no one offered them hospitality, they turned off towards Athens. In those days at Athens all the power was in the hands of Peisistratus, but Miltiades, Cypselus' son, ruled his own property. He came from a family in the 'four-horse chariot' category, and traced his descent from Aeacus and Aegina, but in more recent times he was Athenian, the first member of that family to be Athenian being Philaeus, son of Aeas. This Miltiades, then, was sitting in the forecourt of his house when he saw the Dolonci passing along, wearing foreign dress and carrying spears. He hailed them and when they drew near he offered them lodging and hospitality. This they accepted, and after being entertained by him, they told him all about the oracle; when they had finished their account, they begged him to carry out the divine bidding. Miltiades listened to what they had to say, then immediately acceded to the request. He was far from happy with the regime of Peisistratus, and anxious to be out of it. He at once set out for Delphi to enquire of the oracle whether he should do as the Dolonci had requested.

The priestess of Apollo bade him do so. So it was that Cypselus' son Miltiades, an Olympic champion at the four-horse chariot event, on that occasion took with him any Athenians who volunteered to share in the venture, sailed with the Dolonci, and took possession of the place. Those who had brought him in made him their ruler (tyrant) . . . . [Some time later] Miltiades died childless, and he left his sovereign position and his possessions to Stesagoras, his brother Cimon's son . . . . in the war against the people of Lampsacus Stesagoras was killed, after which his brother, Miltiades, son of Cimon, was sent out by the sons of Peisistratus to take control of the place . . . . it was thus he became master of the Thracian Chersonese.

Herodotus 6.34–9

Herodotus does not go to much trouble to clarify the family relationships: the family in question (the Philaids, or descendants of Philaeus) was one of the most distinguished in Athens, and the historian's readers, or listeners, could be expected to know their relationship. The anecdote is a flashback, its aim being to explain the historic Athenian connections with the region. Miltiades II, the hero of the battle of Marathon, was ruling the peninsula until 493; his uncle, Miltiades I, had been the founder of the Athenian settlement there. Herodotus' account of the settlement throws some light upon his view of the relationship between Peisistratus and his fellow nobles, who were at least potentially his rivals. Miltiades was not happy with the regime, but his colonizing venture obviously enjoyed the co-operation, or the outright support, of the tyrant. In a later chaper (6.103) Herodotus adds some information which suggests that the relationship between the Peisistratids and the Philaids was not good. Cimon, the father of Miltiades II, was banished by Peisistratus; during his exile he was a winner in the chariot event for three Olympiads, driving the same team. He was allowed to return to Athens, but after the death of Peisistratus, Cimon was assassinated; according to Herodotus, on the orders of Peisistratus' successors. Nevertheless Cimon's son, Miltiades II, was sent out by them to rule the colony after his brother Stesagoras had been killed there.

The two overseas ventures, to Sigeum and the Chersonese, are sometimes said to mark a new phase in Athenian foreign policy, marked by a commercial drive to the northeast. But in the first place the Athenian presence in the Sigeum area seems to have gone back to an era before 600 BC: Peisistratus merely revived a failed Athenian colony. Secondly, the ventures, like the trade, seem to have been essentially in private hands (although once Peisistratus the adventurer became Peisistratus the ruler, the distinction between his private, and the public, interest became blurred). One notes that in the case of both settlements the mastery, or ownership, passed from father to son, or uncle to nephew, as if it were private property. This is particularly noticeable in the case of the Chersonese; by permitting Miltiades II to take up his inheritance, instead of installing their own man, the Peisistratids seem to acknowledge the settlement belonged to the family of the Philaids, rather than to the Athenian state. One might conjecture that before the tyranny Athens had no foreign policy, certainly no overseas commercial policy, in spite of later conjectures about Solonian plans in that regard. One should not assume that the Athenian settlements at Sigeum and the Chersonese were necessarily intended to be trading posts, although trade passed through them later on. They were probably, like most Greek colonies, agricultural settlements; but the interest in them shown by adventurers like Peisistratus and Miltiades may be connected with their value as raiding bases. Wherever there is trade in the ancient world, there is piracy; for an adventurer it was much easier to seize the treasure ships of others than to turn trader himself.

XVI GENERAL POLICY

(a) Concentrating on their personal interests and the increase in their private establishments, they [the tyrants] ran the cities with policies of maximum caution. Their actual achievements were negligible,[1] except perhaps in regard to their relations with their immediate neighbours.[2]

Thucydides 1.17

(b) In other respects too the regime did not bear hard upon the masses, nor did it arouse particular resentment. *Noblesse* and good judgement were characteristics of these tyrants [the Peisistratids]: although they extracted from the Athenians no more than one-twentieth of rural production,[3] they established Athens as a fine city,[4] were able to carry on wars, and to meet all due obligations on the religious side.[5] In other regards, the state administration continued to function in accordance with the traditional legal arrangements, except that they took care to ensure that one of their own people was always among the top officials.[6]

Thucydides 6.54.5–6

---

1. 'It may at first sight seem strange that Thucydides should thus belittle the achievements of the tyrants, even the most splendid of them, but we must remember again what Thucydides has in mind—wars on a large scale. . . . He was perfectly well aware of the other services that the Peisistratidai, for example, had rendered Athens.' *HCT*, vol. 1, 127.
2. The exception which Thucydides makes to the general ineffectiveness of the tyrants in external affairs may be a reference to an Athenian success against Thebes in 519 BC, when Plataea sought Athenian aid against Theban pressure. According

to Herodotus (6.108) Athens accepted the Plataean alliance, defeated a Theban force, and advanced the Plataean borders.

3. See Section XIV n.3.

4. The early Greek tyrants were famous for the programmes of great public works on which they embarked (programmes that were dismissed by Aristotle *Pol.* 1313b as intended merely to keep their subjects poor and busy). This building activity coincided with the economic and commercial growth noted by Thucydides (1.13), and seems to be connected with the growth of trade and industry, which caused the need for greater port and market facilities, warehouses, offices, and public and recreational amenities, including the permanent homes of city cults. We may, in addition, concede the likelihood of grandiose buildings, spendid processions and festivals designed mainly to advertise the power and wealth of the regime. The best attested public utility built by the Athenian tyrants was the great Fountain House of nine waterheads (the Enneakrounos), mentioned by Thucydides (2.15.5) and seen in the second century AD by the traveller Pausanias (1.14), but not yet identified with certainty by modern archaeologists. The most ambitious of the public buildings was the huge temple of Olympian Zeus, begun during the tyranny, but not completed until Roman times. The Acropolis hill was held by the tyrants as a citadel (a function it retained until the Persian wars), and may have been the site of a palace and military barracks; it was also the centre of the city cult of Athena, to whom was dedicated the great national festival of the Panathenaea, culminating in the magnificent procession from the agora in the lower city winding up the Sacred Way to the temple on the Acropolis. No less celebrated was the festival of Dionysus, brought to Athens from rural Eleutherae: on the slopes of the Acropolis was built a new temple of Apollo, and in the vicinity were performed the competitions in music, dancing and drama, about which we know so much from the surviving plays of the fifth-century poets. The urbanization of Athens under the tyranny, and the growth of civic and cultural amenities, attracted to Athens architects, sculptors, artists and craftsmen of all kinds, causing a self-sustaining spiral of cultural growth which reached its flower in the following century.

5. The items noted by Thucydides, building programmes, wars, and splendid temples and festivals, all cost a great deal of money, and imply a need for high revenues: the fifth-century Athenian democracy was often accused of plundering the rich in order to raise revenue, and one might expect an autocrat to be no better. Thucydides appears to be stressing the moderation of the tyrants' demands. If one asks where in fact the tyrants did get their money from, the answer would probably be 'from the silver mines'.

6. In Section XV we had an example of collaboration between the ruling house and other nobles in the field of colonization. It seems that such collaboration extended to the highest level of state administration; members of what might be regarded as rival families were permitted or encouraged to share with the tyrants even the highest office, that of the archonship. Such active co-operation supports the view that the tyranny was effectively a continuation of the traditional aristocratic style of government: one house was superior, but it ruled with the backing of other great houses, in spite of temporary quarrels and shifting alliances. But another view of the Athenian tyranny in classical times seems to have been that it safeguarded the interests of, and was supported by, the common man,

and to that extent represented a step towards the democratic state.

Evidence of aristocratic co-operation in high office under the tyrants is preserved in the fragment of a list of chief archons for the years 528–521 BC. (The list is a copy, inscribed in 425 BC, but its authenticity, as a true copy of an original list, is not seriously disputed.) The fragment of the list has been plausibly reconstructed as follows:

[On]eto[rides]	(527–526)
[H]ippia[s]	(526–525)
[K]leisthen[es]	(525–524)
[M]iltiades	(524–523)
[Ka]lliades	(524–522)
[. . .]strat[. . .	(522–521)

Of the reconstructions, those of Hippias, Cleisthenes, Miltiades and Calliades are virtually certain; a daring guess for the last name on the list is [Peisi]strat[us], referring to the grandson of the first tyrant. The dating of the archonships is made possible by a reference in Dionysius of Halicarnassus (*Roman Antiquities* 8.3.1) to the archonship of Miltiades. We know from Aristotle (*AP* 17.1) that Peisistratus died in 528–527: thus the list refers to the early years of his successors, and it is appropriate that his eldest son, Hippias, should figure upon it. The list allows us to interpret the meaning of Thucydides' comment that one of 'their own people' should always be among the top officials; the phrase appears to mean 'the inner ruling group' rather than the narrower meaning of 'the ruling house'. The inclusion on the list of members of other noble families usually regarded as rivals to the Peisistratids (including the later lawgiver Cleisthenes) suggests that although alliances within the ruling group shifted from time to time, as is attested from the varying fortunes of the great houses between 560 and 546, the ruling group itself was an enduring political reality. How dramatic were the changes of fortune of the Alcmaeonid house seems to be demonstrated. Herodotus wrote (1.64) that after the final successful return of Peisistratus the Alcmaeonids fled from Athens; and in 6.123 we hear that they were in exile for the duration of the tyranny. If the archon list is genuine, and has been correctly dated, it seems that Herodotus was wrong, and that Cleisthenes, like Cimon (see Section XV(c)), returned from exile to serve the tyranny; later the Alcmaeonids must have been once more exiled, before making their final triumphal return.

When archaeological evidence directly contradicts literary evidence, as here it appears to do, we are inclined to believe the former against the latter (it should be remembered that the dating of the names on the list is itself to some extent dependent on the literary evidence of Dionysius). Herodotus was the chief source used by Aristotle and others; it is dismaying, to say the least, to find his reliability punctured in this way, and should be a warning against unqualified trust in the authority of literary statements made not only by our sources, but by the sources on which they themselves relied.

On the archon list fragments, see *GHI*, 9–12; T. J. Cadoux, *JHS* 58, 1948, 77–9; Jacoby, *Atthis*, 171–6; C. W. J. Eliot and M. F. McGregor, *Phoenix* 14, 1960, 27–35.

XVII   THE SUCCESSORS

(a) When Peisistratus grew old, and died, still holding the tyranny, it was not Hipparchus, as most people believe, but Hippias, the eldest son, who took over the regime . . . . I can state categorically that Hippias was the oldest and took over control, my knowledge in this case being derived from an unusually good source: but it could also be assumed on the following grounds. Hippias seems to have been the only one of Peisistratus' legitimate sons to have had children of his own, as is evident from the altar, and the tablet placed in the Acropolis commemorating the misdeeds of the tyrants. On this tablet there is no mention of any offspring of Thessalus or Hipparchus, but five of Hippias . . . and his name appears directly after that of his father, not unreasonably, as Hippias was the eldest after him, and held the tyranny.
Thucydides 6.54–5

(b) Peisistratus grew old in office, and died of natural causes in the archonship of Philoneus, thirty-three years after his first coup, nineteen of them in office and the rest in exile. It is accordingly nonsense when they say that he was the lover of Solon, and commanded in the war against Megara for Salamis: it is an impossible chronology, if one takes into account the age of the two men, and the dates of their death. When Peisistratus died, his sons took over the regime after him, and ran the administration along the same lines. He had two sons by his legal wife, Hippias and Hipparchus, and two by the lady from Argos, Iophon and Hegesistratus, also known as Thessalus . . . . Because of their prestige and their age Hippias and Hipparchus were now in control; but Hippias, the elder, a man of public affairs and good judgement, was in charge of the administration. Hipparchus was rather immature, sentimental, and artistic; it was he who brought to Athens the poetic circle that included Anacreon and Simonides.

Aristotle, *AP* 17–18

Throughout the duration of the tyranny the government of Athens was officially in the hands of the archons and the other magistrates: the only *official* power held by the Peisistratids was when they shared the archonship. Their authority was unofficial and unconstitutional; there was no office of tyrant, yet the term was used unofficially to indicate what was thought to be the actual source of power in the state, in contrast to the official façade. The ruling house of the Peisistratids existed in a very real and obvious sense. Their presence on the Acropolis, and their personal armed following, made the reality of their power clear beyond dispute. But whose hand was on the tiller in any particular case was not clear. When the death of Peisistratus removed the head of the ruling house, that position would naturally be taken by the eldest legitimate son, generally agreed to be Hippias. But to be the head of the house did not in this case necessarily mean to be the head of the state: some division of functions such as Aristotle implies, was a possibility. We need not be concerned to find an answer to the dispute about who was the 'official' successor of Peisistratus, since there was no office to succeed to: the historical interest in the dispute lies rather in the light it sheds upon the nebulous character of the Athenian tyranny; even the Athenians themselves were not clear who was their unofficial ruler. But historians, anxious to get the record straight, tended to stress the 'legitimacy' of the succession in terms of who was the eldest son, on the assumption that, as head of house, he did inherit the illegitimate power of his father. Popular ideas on the subject are reflected in a drinking song (see Section XVIII(a)).

XVIII THE ASSASSINATION OF HIPPARCHUS

(a) In myrtle branch I will bear my sword
   Like Harmodios and Aristogeiton
   The day they killed the tyrant
   And made Athens the land of equal rights.

   Dear Harmodios, surely you are not dead,
   You live on, they say, in the islands of the blessed,

Where swift-footed Achilles is,
And goodly Diomedes, Tydeus' son, men say.

In myrtle branch I will bear my sword
Like Harmodios and Aristogeiton,
The day they killed the tyrant, Hipparchus,
At the great festival of Athena.

Your story shall live for ever in our land,
Dear Harmodios and Aristogeiton,
Because you killed the tyrant,
And made Athens the land of equal rights.

Athenaeus 695 A-B

(b) At drinking parties they would sing the so-called Song of Harmodios, which began 'Dear Harmodios, surely you are not dead'. They sang it in honour of Harmodios and Aristogeiton, because they destroyed the tyranny of the Peisistratids.

(A note by a classical commentator on Aristophanes' play, *The Acharnians*, 890.)

(c) Aristogeiton and Harmodios, of the Gephyraioi clan, slew Hipparchus, son of Peisistratus and brother of the tyrant Hippias[1] . . . . after that the Athenians for four more years[2] endured not less, but greater tyranny.

Herodotus 5.55

---

1. Herodotus thus corrects the belief, expressed in the song, that Hipparchus was the tyrant at the time of his assassination.
2. The assassination is thus placed by Herodotus in the year 514 BC.

(d) The Alcmaeonids were as much against the tyrants as he [Callias] was . . . . During the whole period of the tyranny they kept away from the tyrants,[1] and it was thanks to the Alcmaeonids that the Peisistratids lost the tyranny. In my judgement, it was they who were the liberators of Athens, much more than Harmodios and Aristogeiton. For the latter only succeeded in infuriating the other Peisistratids when they killed Hipparchus; and did nothing to end their tyranny.[2]

Herodotus 6.123

---

1. The implication of the Greek phrase is that the Alcmaeonids were in exile for the duration of the tyranny (see Hdt. 1.64). But a reconstructed fragment of an

archon list shows that Cleisthenes himself held the archonship in the year 525–524 BC (see Section XVI(b) n.6).

2. Herodotus thus explicitly corrects the popular view that by the assassination of Hipparchus, Harmodios and Aristogeiton liberated Athens from tyranny.

(e) Equally uncritical is the way people accept the traditions of the past, even the traditions of their own country. In fact most of the Athenians believe that Hipparchus was tyrant when he was killed by Harmodios and Aristogeiton. They are unaware that Hippias, being the eldest of Peisistratus' sons, was in charge, and that Hipparchus and Thessalus were his brothers. Harmodios and Aristogeiton, suspecting on that very day, and on the spur of the moment, that information had been passed to Hippias by one of the conspirators, did not attack Hippias, thinking he was forewarned, but determined to go through with it and strike a blow before they were taken. They waylaid Hipparchus, who was marshalling the procession near the so-called Leokoreion, and killed him.

Thucydides 1.20

Thucydides corrects the popular misconception that it was because Hipparchus was the ruler that the assassins killed him. In the first place, Thucydides points out, Hipparchus was *not* the ruler; secondly, they attacked him rather than Hippias because they believed that the latter had been warned, and was on his guard. The implication is that if they had not so believed (and Thucydides leaves it open whether or not they were correct in their suspicion) they would have killed the real ruler, Hippias.

(f) The Athenian people knew by hearsay that the tyranny of Peisistratus and his sons had hardened towards its end, and what is more, had not been destroyed by themselves or by Harmodios but by the Spartans[1] .... As a matter of fact it was a love affair that prompted the action of Aristogeiton and Harmodios; by explaining it in detail I will prove that the Athenians are no more accurate than other people in what they say about their own tyrants and about their past[2] .... Harmodios was courted by Peisistratus' son, Hipparchus, but rejected his advances, and told Aristogeiton about it. In an anguish of jealousy, and afraid that by his power Hipparchus might succeed, Aristogeiton at once began to plot how he could, with the help of his own influence, bring about the fall of the regime. Meanwhile

Hipparchus, after a second abortive attempt to seduce Harmodios, rejected the idea of violence, but set about humiliating him in some oblique manner . . . . An invitation was issued to Harmodios' sister to take part in a procession; then she was rejected on the grounds that she had never been invited in the first place, as her status disqualified her. Indignant as Harmodios was at this, Aristogeiton was far more enraged, for his sake. All the arrangements were made with those who were to take part in the deed; they waited for the great festival of Athena, the only day on which those of the citizens who were taking part in the procession could assemble under arms without arousing suspicion. The two conspirators were to make the first move, then immediately the rest were to join in the action against the bodyguards. The number of those in the conspiracy had been strictly limited, in the interests of security. They hoped that, at the first sign of action they would be joined by others not involved in the plan, armed as they were. When the festival arrived, Hippias was outside the city wall in the Kerameikos with the guards, arranging how all the details of the procession should proceed. Harmodios and Aristogeiton, already clutching their daggers, were moving in, when they saw one of the conspirators chatting familiarly with Hippias (he was easy of access to everyone). They were seized with panic, believing that they were betrayed and as good as lost. So they decided at all costs to kill, if they could, the man who had wronged them, and for whom they had run such risks. Just as they were, they rushed through the gates, ran into Hipparchus near the so-called Leokoreion, and at once fell upon him recklessly, the one enraged by jealousy, the other by humiliation; they beat him, and killed him. Aristogeiton escaped from the bodyguards for the moment as the crowd surged around; he was later taken, and suffered an unpleasant end. Harmodios was cut down on the spot.

Thucydides 6.54–8

---

1. See Section XIX.
2. Thucydides in this passage repeats in greater detail the view that the assassins did *not* eliminate the ruler, nor end the tyranny, and that their choice of victim was solely a spur-of-the-moment decision, based on their fear that Hippias (the actual ruler) had been forewarned. Thucydides here goes further in expressing the view that the conspiracy was in any case not basically an expression of political dissatisfaction with the regime at all, but originated in the personal relationships between the three men, Hipparchus, Harmodios and Aristogeiton. The resulting personal tensions provoked the assassination, which in turn caused a hardening of the regime, and so helped eventually to topple it: great changes come about

as the ultimate result of a chain of unforeseen consequences arising from trivial actions—a theory of history which was close to the heart of Thucydides. In this instance critics have detected a certain inconsistency in his own account. For although the anger of the two assassins against Hipparchus was based on personal, not political, grounds, Aristogeiton did, according to Thucydides, in fact hope to topple the regime: we may guess that it was political, rather than personal, hostility that motivated their supporters and those who were expected to join in the riot, once the first blow was struck. It is also strange that, although the quarrel was with Hipparchus, it was Hippias whom they planned to kill; and yet sheer accident brought it about that they did in fact assassinate Hipparchus, who was the real target of their hatred.

Herodotus and Thucydides agree that the assassination did not end the regime. Nevertheless Athenian tradition persisted in regarding Harmodios and Aristogeiton as the liberators of Athens from tyranny, at least in the sense that they had sacrificed their lives in the cause of freedom. Statues were erected to their memory at public expense, and their kinsmen were granted public honours in perpetuity. The statues were later removed by the Persians and taken off to Susa: after the Persian war was over a fresh group of statues was made and set up in the agora. Alexander the Great recovered the originals and returned them to Athens, where they were re-erected near their replacements, and were seen by Pausanias (1.8.5). The 'human interest' in the story of the affair helped to preserve and embellish it, so that it became a legend in Athens. Thucydides' attempt to strip away the heroic and romantic elements then fixed it in the written record as one of the best-known episodes in the history of sixth-century Athens.

Aristotle included the story in *AP* (ch. 18), following the account of Thucydides, but departing from it in two details. On the question of who actually was *the* tyrant at the time of the assassination, Aristotle expresses the belief that the two eldest sons of Peisistratus, Hippias and Hipparchus, shared the responsibility, but that the senior, Hippias, was in charge of administration (see Section XVII(b)). Secondly, Aristotle stated that it was Thessalus, a younger brother, who was the suitor of Harmodios, and so indirectly the cause of the conspiracy. By his detailed refutation of the popular version, which made the assassination of 'the tyrant Hipparchus' the decisive element in the fall of the tyranny, Thucydides had tried to debunk what he regarded as a falsification of history. But the official honours paid to the *tyrannicides* (as they were officially described) indicated that the popular misconception was in fact the officially approved version. By his view that Hipparchus was, if not *the* tyrant, at least a partner in the ruling house, Aristotle justified the official view that the assassins *were* in fact tyrant-slayers. By substituting Thessalus for Hipparchus as the suitor of Harmodios, Aristotle, or, more probably, a source used by Aristotle, denied that the murder of Hipparchus was directly the result of the abortive love affair. In the controversy there were political implications for fifth-century Athenian politics. As in the case of Cylon and the family curse, so with the assassination, the reputation of the Alcmaeonids was involved. The view of Herodotus and Thucydides was that the Alcmaeonids bore much of the credit for the liberation of Athens from tyranny; the legend of the tyrannicides undermined this credit. The whole controversy illustrates the importance of family feuds in Athenian public life, and the influence of family tradition upon Athenian historiography.

XIX   THE END OF THE TYRANNY

(a) Hippias was now tyrant; he became increasingly bitter against the Athenians because of the death of Hipparchus.[1] The Alcmaeonids, an Athenian family banished by the Peisistratids,[2] attempted, together with the other Athenian exiles, to force a return, but without success; they were badly mauled in an attempt to return and liberate Athens after fortifying Leipsydrion, above Paeonia.[3] So then, determined to use any means to hit at the Peisistratids, they took a contract from the Amphictioni[4] to complete the temple at Delphi which still stands there, but at that time did not yet exist. The Alcmaeonids were men of wealth and came from an old and distinguished line; when the temple was finished, it was grander than the planned specifications, and whereas the latter had provided for freestone construction, they added a façade of Parian marble.[5]

According to the Athenian version, these men, during their stay in Delphi, bribed the priestess of Apollo: whenever any of the ruling caste of Sparta should come to consult the oracle on any matter, private or public, she was to bid them to liberate Athens. When the Spartans received this injunction over and over again, they sent Anchimolios,[6] Aster's son . . . with an army, to drive out the Peisistratids, in spite of the fact that the latter were their best friends; for to them the divine will had priority above mere human considerations. This task force was sent by sea; the commander put in to Phaleron and disembarked his troops. But the Peisistratids had intelligence of this in advance, and summoned help from Thessaly in accordance with the alliance between them. The Thessalians responded to their appeal by sending, as agreed, a thousand horse and their king Cineas of Conia. Reinforced by these allies, the Peisistratids devised the following strategem: they cleared the ground all round Phaleron for a cavalry charge, then they sent in the cavalry against the encamped force. The charge inflicted heavy losses on the Spartans; Anchimolios was among the casualties. The survivors, now hemmed in near the ships, withdrew. That was the end of the first Spartan intervention. The tomb of Anchimolios lies in Alopeke in Attica, near the temple of Heracles in Kynosarges.

The Spartans subsequently fitted out another expeditionary force on a larger scale, and sent it to Athens after officially designating as commander their king, Cleomenes, Anaxandrides' son; this time it went not by sea but overland. The invading force first encountered the

Thessalian cavalry, which was soon routed with a loss of over forty men. The remainder retreated as best they could, by the direct road into Thessaly. Cleomenes entered Athens together with the Athenian freedom fighters, drove the tyrants back to the Pelasgian wall,[7] and cornered them.

There was in fact no chance of the Spartans flushing out the Peisistratids; the former had no intention of settling down to a blockade, whereas the latter were well supplied with food and water. After a few days' siege the Spartans would have withdrawn back to Sparta, but fortunately for them, and unfortunately for the Peisistratids,[8] their children were captured as they were being conveyed out of the country. This upset all their plans; in exchange for their children they agreed to the terms offered by the Athenians, that is, to leave Attica within five days. Subsequently they left for Sigeum on the river Scamander. The regime had lasted for thirty-six years.[9]

Herodotus 5.62–5

---

1. Apart from one note in *AP* chapter 16 (see Section XIV), to the effect that the regime deteriorated after the death of Peisistratus, the Athenian tradition which Herodotus, Thucydides and Aristotle all followed indicated that only after the assassination of Hipparchus, that is in the last four years of a thirty-six year regime, did the Athenian tyranny show those traits of despotic repression which were regarded as the hallmark of that type of government. The tradition appears elsewhere explicitly, for example in a dialogue attributed to Plato:

   > After the death of Hipparchus, for three years the Athenians endured the tyranny under his brother Hippias. The older folk used to say that *only for those years* was there a true tyranny in Athens: for the rest of the time the Athenians lived in a sort of Golden Age.
   >
   > [Plato] *Hipparchus* 229 b

   Folklore seems to have preserved more or less only pleasant or amusing anecdotes about the regime until 514 BC, and nothing at all about changes to the form or machinery of government. Later historians had then to explain why, in that case, the fall of the tyranny was regarded as a liberation, and the name of the 'tyrannicides' honoured. The two legends (the Golden Age of the tyrants, and the liberation from tyranny) could be harmonized only by the assumption of some drastic change in the exercise of the tyrants' power. The cause for such a change was found in the aftermath of the assassination which, it could have been reasoned, turned Hippias from an easy-going, good-natured man (Thuc.6.57.2) into a bloodthirsty despot.

2. See Section XVI n.6.

3. There is no place in Attica identified by this name: Aristotle seems here to have corrected Herodotus' geography, see (b) n.2. A point to be noted in the

64

drinking song which commemorated the defeat at Leipsydrion is the reference to the 'men of high degree' (the Eupatrids). The tone of the song implies that the attempt to 'liberate' Athens was far from being a popular movement, but rather an adventure by a rival group of the nobility, the result of a split in the traditional ruling élite of Attica.

4. The sanctuary of Apollo at Delphi was under the protection of a council of the twelve tribes of northeast Greece, the so-called Amphictionic Council.

5. Herodotus has already (1.50 and 2.180) referred to the fire which destroyed the temple in 548 BC. The Amphictionic Council raised the money for the rebuilding by asking for donations from many quarters, including Egypt. A comment by an early scholar on the text of Demosthenes 21.1.44 says that the Alcmaeonid Megacles took ten silver talents, spent three on the construction, and used the other seven to pay troops and persuade the Spartans to send help against Athens. Another comment, on the 7th Pythian Ode of Pindar, says, citing Philochorus as source, that when they were in exile the Alcmaeonids vowed to rebuild the temple, and fulfilled that vow after their return to Athens. Both Herodotus and Aristotle imply that the Alcmaeonids misused the funds entrusted to them for the rebuilding.

6. The name is corrected by Aristotle to Anchimolos.

7. Usually known as the Mycenaean wall, it dates from the thirteenth century BC; its construction converted the Acropolis into a citadel. Its width varied from 3.6 to 6 metres, and its height has been calculated at from 8 to 10 metres (Hopper, *The Acropolis*, 27).

8. Herodotus stresses the element of chance in the historical consequences (as Thucydides did in the affair of the assassination). What the Spartans might or would have done is presumably an inference by the historian.

9. 'The third longest tyranny was that of the Peisistratids at Athens. It was not continuous, for twice during his period of tyranny Peisistratus was in exile: during the period of thirty-three years he actually ruled as tyrant for seventeen, and his sons for eighteen, so that the total period of their rule was thirty-five years.'

Aristotle, Politics 1315b 30–4

For Aristotle's reckoning in *AP* see (b) n.3.

(b) After this [conspiracy] the regime became much harsher. Reprisals for the death of his brother included the liquidation of many, and the exile of others; Hippias trusted no one, and ruled with an iron hand. About three years after the death of Hipparchus, the situation in Athens had deteriorated. Hippias began to fortify Munychia, with the idea of making it his base.[1] It was at this stage that he was driven out by the Spartan king, Cleomenes. A stream of oracular responses had been bidding the Spartans to put an end to the tyranny; the background was as follows. The exiles, of whom the most prominent were the Alcmaeonids, were unable to force a return by themselves, after many failures. Among their unsuccessful enterprises had been the fortification of Leipsydrion, in the area below Mount Parnes.[2] They had been joined by some men from the city of Athens, but the tyrants besieged and captured the position. This is the fiasco to which they referred in the lines:

O Leipsydrion, graveyard of the partisans!
Such men they were that you destroyed -
heroes and men of high degree.
That day they showed the stock from which they came.

After failing in all other ways, they took up a contract to build the temple at Delphi. They did very well out of it, and with the funds they managed to enlist the help of the Spartans. Whenever men came from Lacedaemon to consult the oracle, the priestess of Apollo would invariably reply that they should liberate Athens. Finally she talked them into it, in spite of the fact that there were close ties between the Peisistratids and Sparta. An additional factor in the Spartan decision was the friendship of the Peisistratids for Argos. The first attempt was the dispatch of Anchimolos with a task force by sea. He was defeated and killed when the Thessalian Cineas with a thousand cavalry came to the assistance of the Athenian defence. This enraged the Spartans, who then sent their king, Cleomenes, with a more ambitious force overland. He defeated the Thessalian cavalry who were blocking his way into Attica, drove Hippias into a position behind the so-called Pelasgian wall, and, with the help of some Athenians, besieged him there. While the siege was in progress, the children of the Peisistratids were captured while trying to escape. It was in consequence of this that the Peisistratids made a deal, to save their chidren: within five days they evacuated all their possessions and handed over the Acropolis to the Athenians. It was the year when Harpactides was archon. They had held the tyranny for about seventeen years since their father's death. The total duration of the regime, including that of their father, was forty-nine years.[3]

Aristotle, *AP* 19

---

1. Munychia is one of the small harbours lying west of the bay of Phaleron. Behind the harbour is high ground which acted as a natural protection to the harbour from land assault. The plan of Hippias was to improve on the natural position in order to make it as far as possible unassailable by land, like a sea castle. Such a plan implied that the garrison had command of the sea; otherwise it could have been a death trap. This fortification is one of the several pieces of information which Aristotle adds to the narrative of his source, Herodotus. Further additional information supplied by him includes (a) the text of the drinking song, (b) the

friendship of the Peisistratids for Argos as one motive for the Spartan decision to invade, and (c) the dating of the regime's fall by the archon-year.
2. Note the correction of Herodotus' geography.
3. Aristotle includes the periods of exile in the total period of the tyranny, which by his reckoning should add up to a half-century (560–510 BC). What kind of regime existed at Athens during the exiles of the tyrants is a mystery on which the tradition was silent. But apparently archons continued to be appointed, as if nothing had happened. In trying to reconstruct any kind of history of the sixth century we are hampered not only by the extreme paucity of recorded material, but also because the first history of Athens that survives, the *AP*, is concerned with constitutional forms, not with the more difficult problem of the real distribution of power in the community, and how that power was actually exerted. It took Thucydides, in his enigmatic comment on Pericles (2.65), explicitly to contrast the theory of the constitution with the reality of influence in the decision-making process. Thucydides was also the only historian to hint how the power of the tyrants was converted into political action, when he remarked that they ensured that one of their people was always in high office. It need hardly be said that, by itself, this provision would not have sufficed to maintain an autocratic rule which included, as we hear almost incidentally, the banishment and execution of suspected opponents, and the arrest of their children to provide hostages for their conduct.

XX   THE COMPETITION FOR POWER AT ATHENS

(a) Great as Athens had been before, rid of the tyrants, she now became yet greater.[1] In Athens there were two leading men—Cleisthenes the Alcmaeonid, the one who was supposed to have bribed the priestess of Apollo, and Isagoras, Tisandrus' son, a man of notable lineage . . . . These men were locked in conflict over political power and, when Cleisthenes was losing ground, he turned to the demos for support.[2] Later he changed the Athenians from a four-tribe into a ten-tribe people,[3] abandoning the [tribal] names called after the sons of Ion . . . and making up new names, after heroes, all of them native to Athens except Ajax whom he counted as a close connection, being a neighbour and ally.[4] In this, Cleisthenes was, as I see it, following the example of his uncle, the Cleisthenes who had been tyrant of Sicyon . . . . The latter changed the names of the Dorian tribes, so that they should not be the same as the tribes of Sicyon and Argos . . . . Well, in my opinion, the Athenian Cleisthenes imitated his uncle and namesake because, like him, he despised the Ionians, and did not want the [Athenian] tribes to be the same as the Ionian.[5] For when he had drawn to his own faction the demos, which had before been completely left out of everything, he changed the names of the [Athenian] tribes, and increased their number: he created ten tribe-leaders where there had been four, and rearranged the demes among the tribes in ten parts.[6] By the adhesion of the demos Cleisthenes became much stronger than his opponents.

Isagoras was now, in his turn, on the losing side, and countered with the following strategem. He called in the Spartan Cleomenes, with whom he had close ties ever since the siege of the Peisistratids. (Gossip said that there was something between Cleomenes and Isagoras' wife.) The first thing that Cleomenes did was to send to Athens, demanding the expulsion of Cleisthenes and many of his group, saying that they were 'accursed'.[7] This is what he said in his message, on the instruction of Isagoras. (The Alcmaeonids and their faction were held responsible for the murder; but he and his friends had no part in it.) . . . So it was that Cleomenes sent to expel Cleisthenes and the 'accursed'. Cleisthenes himself slipped out of Athens; but this did not prevent Cleomenes coming to Athens with a small escort, and banishing as 'accursed' 700 Athenian families, suggested by Isagoras. As his second move Cleomenes then tried to dissolve the council and hand over the government to a body of 300, supporters of Isagoras.[8] But the council stood firm, and declined to co-operate. Cleomenes, together with Isagoras and his group, then seized the Acropolis. The rest of the Athenians then joined forces and blockaded them for two days. On the third day, after a deal had been made, the Spartan members of the garrison left the country . . . as for the rest, the Athenians held them under close arrest pending execution . . . they were subsequently put to death.[9] After that the Athenians recalled Cleisthenes and the 700 families driven out by Cleomenes. They also sent a deputation to Sardis, seeking an alliance with the Persians, for they realized that what they had done had put them in a state of war with Cleomenes and the Spartans. When the deputation reached Sardis and delivered their message, Artaphrenes, son of Hystaspes, the viceroy of Sardis, asked them what manner of men they were and where in the world did they dwell, that they sought to become allies of the Persians. When he heard their answer, he curtly informed them that, if the Athenians gave to King Darius earth and water, he for his part would deal with them:[10] if they did not, he bade them be gone. The delegates, acting on their own inititative, said they would give it; they were indeed eager for the alliance. But when they returned to their own land they found themselves in deep trouble.

Herodotus 5.66–73

1. It would be perhaps unwise to attach too much weight to this introductory sentence, for it is difficult to see in what literal sense Athens could have been regarded as one of the great Greek states in the sixth century. In his historical introduction Thucydides discussed the growth in wealth and power of the early Greek states, using as an index the size of the war fleets they built. From this point of view he rated as important powers the Ionian states (before they were overrun by Persia), also Samos, Phocaea and Corcyra: of Athens he says (1.14) that she possessed a few vessels, mainly of the fifty-oared (old-fashioned) type. (Needless to say, this is only one way of measuring greatness.) Herodotus himself had written in 1.59 of how the Lydian king Croesus had learned of Attica under the tyranny that it was 'held down and torn apart by Peisistratus' (an impression which is, incidentally, distinctly at variance with the Golden Age image of later folklore). In the passage (see Section XX above) describing the reception of the Athenian delegation at Sardis it appears that the Persians had never heard of Athens.

2. As in previous accounts of Athenian history before the tyranny, so now politics at Athens is represented, in general, as a tug-of-war between a handful of rich men. The student of history would naturally wonder whether the situation was so represented because, a hundred years later, when the history of the time began to be written, the complications of various interest groups and social and economic pressures had been forgotten, and history had become simplified to the clash of personalities. On the other hand there is also the possibility that the realities of politics *were* these personal ambitions and power clashes. One point in favour of the latter view is that all our sources agree that the machinery of government associated with the democratic style, popular participation, elected or balloted magistrates and so forth, worked as well under an autocratic type of government as it did in what was regarded as a genuine democracy; so presumably the secret of democracy was not in the machinery, but in how, and by whom, it was operated. In this passage Herodotus introduces what he apparently regarded as an entirely new factor in the politics of Athens, the city demos itself. Perhaps this was the view prevailing in Athens when Herodotus was writing (in the second half of the fifth century); the view differs sharply from that implied by the later reconstruction of Aristotle, who regarded the popular movement as a political factor predating Solon.

3. For the meaning of this enigmatic statement see Section XXI below.

4. Ajax was associated with the island of Salamis, which had in the sixth century been brought under the dominion of Athens. A decree concerned with the settlement of an Athenian colony on Salamis in the late sixth century survives: *GHI*, 25–7.

5. This whole retrospect of early Athenian history is, from the point of view of Herodotus' narrative, merely an aside to explain how Athens came to be involved with the Persians in the first place. Thus the reforms of Cleisthenes are peripheral to the subject, and can be dismissed in a brief reference. In contrast, Herodotus enlarges on the motives of Cleisthenes for renaming the Attic 'tribes' because they form part of a tale which his listeners would find amusing for its 'human interest'.

6. The received text at this point hardly makes sense as it stands: the phrase may be an explanatory insertion interpolated by a copyist; or the text may be corrupt.

The meaning remains obscure: the translation offered is from an emended text.

7. See Section I(b).

8. The incident was included in Aristotle's *AP* (see XXI below), following Herodotus almost word for word. The narrative is puzzling, and leaves much unsaid. Although Cleisthenes is winning, and has made himself stronger than his opponents by the support of the city demos, a message from Sparta is enough to make him abandon the struggle and withdraw; then Cleomenes arrives 'with a small escort', and is able to expel 700 families (at least three or four thousand people). This is done at the word of a Spartan king, advised by Isagoras, with no constitutional procedure that we hear of, and on a flimsy pretext, for it is difficult to take seriously the charge that not only the Alcmaeonid family, but 700 families had been contaminated by the 'curse'. The legal and constitutional arrangements at Athens are ignored or suspended, until Cleomenes begins to interfere with the council. But which council is meant? The old Council of the Areopagus, whose functions included the duty of protecting the constitution? The Solonian Council of Four Hundred (if there was one)? Or a new council set up by Cleisthenes? See Section XXI n. 3.

9. The obvious implication of Herodotus' words here, namely that Isagoras and his supporters were excluded from the safe conduct, held under close arrest, and then executed, is subsequently contradicted by Herodotus himself (5.74, see Section XXIII(a) n. 1), and is corrected by Aristotle in the light of documentary evidence (*AP* 20, see Section XX(b) n. 3).

10. The gift of earth and water to the Persians was the symbol of submission. The assent of the Athenian delegates to this demand made Athens, in Persian terms, a state subject to the Great King: the Persian satrap apparently took the Athenian delegates' word for the compact, and the subsequent unilateral repudiation of the deal by the Athenian home government could not be expected to cancel the agreement, even if the Persians heard about the repudiation. Thus, when Athenians later intervened in the Ionian revolt on the side of the rebels in 499 BC, the act placed Athens in the position of rebellious subject, and liable to the reprisals that followed. This is the connecting point with Herodotus' main line of causation in his account of how the great clash of civilizations began. The political turmoil at Athens and the Spartan interventions there, so important for the historians of Athens, are quite subsidiary to Herodotus' narrative, and treated rather carelessly. Unfortunately, as the first written account (?) of the events it was Herodotus' version that formed the basis for later reconstructions.

(b) After the liquidation of the tyranny a factional struggle broke out between Isagoras, Teisander's son, a friend of the tyrants,[1] and Cleisthenes, of the Alcmaeonid clan. When he was losing ground in the party struggle, Cleisthenes brought over the demos to his following, [thus] handing over political control to the masses.[2] Feeling his position undermined, Isagoras invited back to Athens Cleomenes, with whom he had personal ties, and persuaded him jointly to 'drive out the curse'. (The Alcmaeonids were regarded as being among the 'accursed'.) When Cleisthenes withdrew, Cleomenes, with a meagre following, ceremoniously expelled 700 Athenian households. When this had been completed, he set about liquidating the council, and installing Isagoras and 300 of his friends as controllers of the city. But when the council resisted, and the masses took to the streets, Cleomenes, Isagoras, and their group took refuge in the Acropolis. The demos took up positions, and blockaded them for two days. On the third day they allowed Cleomenes and all those with him to depart under safe conduct;[3] then they sent for Cleisthenes and all the other exiles. With the demos now in control of the situation,[4] Cleisthenes was their leader, and 'champion of the people'. For it was the Alcmaeonids who had more or less been the decisive element in the expulsion of the tyrants, and they had for the most part persisted in their opposition to them.

Aristotle, AP 20

---

1. A comment interpolated by Aristotle into what is almost a transcription of Herodotus' narrative; because Aristotle's account follows Herodotus so closely, the divergences stand out as the more significant. But in this case the reason for the interpolation is not at first sight clear. As far as collaboration with the tyrants was concerned, the same might have been said about the Alcmaeonids and other notable Athenian families. But tradition saw the situation at Athens following the fall of the tyranny as primarily a series of political manoeuvres between Cleisthenes and Isagoras, the former cast in the role of the liberator and founder of the future democracy, the latter epitomizing reaction, including collaboration with repression, oligarchy, treason and finally the desire to make himself tyrant (see Section XXII).
2. Aristotle's interpretation of Cleisthenes' action in turning to the demos for support is more dramatic than any expressed by Herodotus. Hitherto the political struggle has been seen as one of personal followings – the commoners are involved more or less as extras on a stage dominated by the principals. But Cleisthenes, by widening the conflict to involve in his cause the demos which hitherto had been *totally excluded* (Hdt. 5.66), took a decisive step which was to end in an unexpected result – the surrender of political control to the urban masses. Thus Aristotle inserts into the 'news columns' of Herodotus' narrative an editorial comment which sums up, not the substance of Cleisthenes' immediate reforms, but Aristotle's view of their historical importance in the light of Athenian political development.
3. Aristotle here appears to be contradicting Herodotus' statement about the fate of Isagoras and his supporters when Cleomenes surrendered to the Athenians besieging the Acropolis (see Section XX(a) n. 9). But the apparent contradiction merely corrects the false implication of Herodotus' rather careless wording: the latter knew that Isagoras had not on this occasion been executed, for he makes him reappear later in the narrative (5.74 see Section XXIII). In this particular instance we may hope to perceive something of Aristotle's methods, and the grounds on which the correction was made. In a note on a passage of Aristophanes'

play, *Lysistrata*, line 273, an ancient scholar wrote:

> Cleomenes . . . who had been besieged by the Athenians and been allowed
> to withdraw under safe conduct, went home, then [later] he held Eleusis [in
> Attica]. When Cleomenes' supporters were occupying Eleusis, the Athenians
> demolished their houses and seized as public property their possessions; upon
> their persons they passed the death sentence. This they inscribed on a bronze
> plaque, and set it up by the old temple.

The note perhaps preserves the actual wording of the inscription on the plaque,
which would have been easily accessible to Aristotle and his sources. It was the
clearest evidence that Isagoras and his supporters were sentenced to death as
collaborators with the Spartan invaders on the occasion of the invasion sent to
avenge Cleomenes' earlier submission after the siege of the Acropolis. Isagoras
was, in other words, sentenced to death at a later date by a public decree, on
the grounds of treason, not summarily executed after the siege.

4. The scenario is one of open revolution, with the city masses apparently out of
hand. The narrative indicates that in Aristotle's reading of the situation the
initiative lay with the crowd: it was the urban masses who made Cleisthenes
their champion. The era when politics at Athens consisted mainly of private
feuds between the leaders of society was over.

XXI   THE REFORMS OF CLEISTHENES

These were the grounds on which the demos put its trust in Cleisthenes:
at that time he stood at the head of the masses. Three years had passed
since the end of the tyranny, and Isagoras was archon.[1] Cleisthenes' first
move was to reassign all the citizens into ten 'tribes' instead of the previous
four: his aim was to mix them all together, so that more would be assimilated
into the running of the state.[2] This is the origin of the saying, 'No
discrimination by tribe', as an answer to any move to raise the question
of a man's ancestry. Secondly, Cleisthenes brought into being a Council
of Five Hundred in place of the Four Hundred;[3] each tribe was to contribute
fifty men, whereas hitherto there had been a hundred [from each tribe].
The reason why he chose not to allocate them into twelve tribes was to
avoid the allocation being on the basis of the already existing *trittyes*, for
there were twelve *trittyes* in the four tribes . . . . [If this had happened] the
aim of assimilating the masses into the total mix would have been frustrated.
He divided up the land of Attica into thirty parts, grouping the demes:
of these thirty parts ten were in the city area, ten in the coastal area, and
ten in the inland. It was these thirty parts that he termed the *trittyes*, and
he allotted three to each tribe, in such a way that each tribe should be

represented in all three [geographical] areas.[4] He made all who lived in each of the demes fellow-demesmen. This was to avoid the practice of calling each other by their fathers' names, which would have exposed the newly enfranchised citizens. People were to be known by [the names of] their demes, which is why in fact the Athenians do now so call themselves. Cleisthenes also created the [office of] demarchs, having the same functions as those hitherto performed by the naucrari: what he did in fact was to replace the naucraries by the demes.[5] Some of the latter he named after their localities, some after their founders; for not all [the demes] had a local identity. The clans, the brotherhoods and the priesthoods he left to retain their traditional functions. He named the tribes after ten heroes, the choice being made by the priestess of Apollo [at Delphi] from a pre-selected list of 100 founders.

Aristotle, AP 21

---

1. Aristotle's account at this point parts from that of Herodotus, which from now turns to the contacts of Athens with Persia. Before embarking on a summary of Cleisthenes' reforms, Aristotle mentions (a) the grounds for the mass support for Cleisthenes, that is, the Alcmaeonid record of opposition to the tyrants, and (b) the date of the reforms, which he does with unusual care, citing both the archon-year (508–507), and the interval since the end of the tyranny (three years). Since the reforms were the expression of Cleisthenes' dramatic conversion to the popular cause, we must date this conversion *before* them and we may guess that the setback to Cleisthenes' career (when he realized that he was losing the struggle against Isagoras) was the election of Isagoras to the archonship. But Aristotle's chronology of events – the election, the conversion, Isagoras' invitation to Cleomenes, the expulsion of the Alcmaeonids, the arrival of Cleomenes, his attack upon the council, the riots, the surrender, and the return of Cleisthenes – seem to imply that the reforms were carried out *at the end* of this sequence, that is, when Isagoras had already left Athens under the truce. We can assume that Aristotle is right about the archon-year; whether or not he was able to consult a copy of the actual law, he was certain that its official dating was to the archonship of Isagoras. But it seems in the highest degree unlikely that Cleisthenes' elaborate electoral arrangements could have been carried out in the remnant of the archon-year remaining after the expulsion of the Spartan garrison; and indeed there must have been more pressing things to be done at this critical time. It is usually assumed that Cleisthenes proposed a motion in the assembly foreshadowing the intention of the later reform, when Isagoras was still archon, and *before* the Spartan intervention. The sequence of events in Aristotle's account is confused because he follows the narrative of his source (Herodotus) until the end of its relevance for his subject, and only then proceeds to discuss the reforms themselves. Apparently Cleisthenes felt able to bring forward as a private individual in the assembly radical constitutional proposals in the face of the opposition of his rival as chief magistrate; this in turn implies that the city masses, if not yet out of

hand, were far from powerless when they met as an assembly, even in face of aristocratic opposition, that is, that a kind of revolution had already taken place even before the reforms had come into effect, and that the latter recognized a redistribution of power which was already a political reality. The motion of Cleisthenes foreshadowing the reforms was dated to the archonship of Isagoras, but their implementation must be regarded as taking place some time later. Apart from the time needed to fix the complex details of the tribal reform, the theoretical, almost academic, style of the proposed changes seems more in keeping with a calm and unhurried atmosphere than with the turbulent scenes that have been described above.

2. The expression used by Aristotle is, literally translated, 'wishing that more could participate in the *politeia*' (the constitution). It is not clear whether Aristotle meant 'so that more people could *possess citizenship*', or 'so that more could take *part in running the state*'; the latter interpretation of course includes the former, and the former implies the latter. Aristotle makes it very clear that in his view Cleisthenes' primary purpose in effecting the tribal reforms was to assimilate into the (running of the) state men who, although living permanently in Attica, were not yet recognized members of the state. It was not enough to give them the privileges of co-citizenship, he wished to assimilate them without trace; but this was hampered by the fact that they had no status in the old tribes, as they stood outside the clan and phratry system, hence (a) the inauguration of the new tribes, based on local residence, and unconnected with the old clan and phratry system, and (b) the taboo on discriminating among citizens by their tribal affiliations or the lack of them. But why was it so important for Cleisthenes and his group to bring new citizens into the running of the state? We do not know, and many scholars doubt whether Aristotle is right in so interpreting Cleisthenes' intentions. But the author of *Politics* certainly did believe that it was a policy of radical politicians to extend their support base by introducing new citizens:

> Such a democracy will find useful devices such as those used by Cleisthenes, when he wished to increase the democracy . . . that is, more and new tribes and phratries must be created, and the celebration of private rites should be consolidated into a smaller number of public ones. Everything should be done to foster the mixture of all together, and to dissolve the preceding associations.

Aristotle, *Politics* 1319b 20–8

The implication in the above extract, namely that Cleisthenes interfered with the organization of the phratries, is doubtful, and seems to be denied in *AP* 21. But the *Politics* passage confirms that in Aristotle's view the tribal reform was intended to achieve two objects: (a) to enlarge the citizen body by the admission of new citizens, without disturbing the harmony of the community by creating distinctions between old and new citizens; and (b) to break up patterns of loyalty which might stand in the way of change, and so prevent the new 'mix' from working as it should.

3. Aristotle gives no details of any changes affecting the duties and powers of the magistrates, nor of the new council. It seems that, in his view, the new council functioned much as it did in the later period; basically, that is, it acted as a steering committee for the assembly, scrutinizing and preparing all business before it

was submitted to them. Aristotle regarded such a body as essential to the functioning of any democratic state; the final decision lay with the people meeting in the ecclesia, but preliminary discussion in the council was necessary to select business and to define issues. The need for such a committee implies the sovereignty of the assembly in fact, as well as in theory, and the inauguration of the new council by Cleisthenes at this time fits well the idea that the revolution which ejected the archon (Isagoras) and his Spartan allies marks a sharp change in the power structure, when the urban masses made their power felt, and became a factor henceforth to be reckoned with. But Aristotle's concentration on changes in the *forms* of government, rather than on the power divisions in the state, in this case gives the impression that the formation of the new council was a routine measure, consequent on the reorganization of the citizen body into ten new tribes. One might assume from Aristotle's account that the new Council of Five Hundred simply replaced that of Four Hundred, set up by Solon (assuming that such a council *was* set up by Solon), and continued in its functions. This would again imply that the democratic style of government, with the demos in effective control, went back to Solon, and that no real change in the distribution of political influence preceded the Cleisthenic reforms. On the face of it, not a very convincing scenario. There is one other factor to be taken into account. During the tyranny the government of all Attica had tended to become centralized in the city of Athens, and the increased control was shown in the development of new functions, such as those of taxation and regional courts, operating from Athens. Control from the centre meant an apparatus of officials with delegated authority to ensure that the will of the tyrant was carried out (the circuit judges are the only such officials actually mentioned in the tradition). When the tyranny fell, the personal apparatus of the tyrants disappeared, together with their hired bodyguards; but unless the centralization of administration also disappeared, the functions of the tyrants' officials were taken over by others. It is now perhaps that the participatory style of Athenian democracy really began. Paid soldiers were replaced by citizen hoplites; the civic apparatus of the tyrants was replaced by the voluntary and unpaid labour of citizens. In the case of the council, each tribal delegation of fifty men was on full-time duty in Athens for one-tenth of the year (a *prytany*), thus effectively replacing the permanent entourage of the tyrants. No doubt their duties accumulated with the growth of public business. In classical times, in the view of an eminent scholar, the committee was empowered to 'give instructions to the magistrates, to supervise them and co-operate with them, to direct diplomatic negotiations, and to control the finances of the state' (De Sanctis, *Atthis*, 347). We should not think of the creation of the new council as a routine measure, consequent upon the tribal reform, with all the administrative changes which came with it. The new council was the visible sign of a fresh system of government, operated in a democratic way by voluntary, short-term, and unpaid officials, recruited at grass-roots level in the demes.

4. The so-called tribal reform involved a reorganization of the citizen body, including the new citizens, for the purposes of administration, political activity and military service. The reorganization of the people was accomplished by grouping the demes, or parishes, in which they lived, into larger units, the *trittys*; the *trittyes* were then grouped together to form the new *tribes*, or electoral divisions. A master plan recognized three main areas of Attica: they were (1) the city of Athens, its

plain, and all the area between the city and the coast, including the coastal area itself; (2) the other coastal areas with their immediate hinterland; and (3) the rest of Attica, that is, the inland. (The island of Salamis was not included in the plan, and Athenian citizens who lived there were recognized as belonging to a deme in Attica itself; that is, they were treated as Athenians settled 'abroad', or as colonists.) For the purposes of the plan each of the main areas was regarded as consisting of ten sections or sub-areas (the *trittyes*), making thirty *trittyes* in all. They might include anything from one to ten demes, depending on population. On the basis of these quite artificial and theoretical *territorial* divisions, the new *population* units (the new tribes) were formed. Every tribe included one city, one coastal, and one inland *trittys*. Thus the reoganization grouped demes and clusters of demes into an entirely new administrative pattern which cut across traditional lines of association: the most striking break-up of a natural pattern of association was the city of Athens itself, which was cut, together with its environs, into ten units. Without any movement of population whatever, a total reorganization left citizens associated for administrative purposes with men from other parts of the country, while neighbours in the city area could find themselves in a different tribe to those living in the next street. Modern research has filled in details of the organization, confirming Aristotle's description. But the reasons that he believed to be at the bottom of the reorganization are disputed.

Since Athenian tradition for long regarded Cleisthenes as the founder of Athenian democracy, it is not surprising that *demokratia* (people-power) was regarded as the central aim of his reforms. But it is always dangerous to assume that results necessarily coincide with aims: Cleisthenes' motives are a matter of guesswork for historians; any informed guess should take note of the circumstances prevailing at the time of the reforms, and the problems which demanded immediate action. We cannot rate these problems in the order of urgency in which they appeared to Cleisthenes, but they included (a) the possibility that a new tyranny would be set up, either by the return of the Peisistratids or by an ambitious strong man like Isagoras, (b) a prevailing state of political lawlessness such as to threaten that the unified state of Athens might disintegrate into warring enclaves commanded by rival dynasts, each basing his power upon a local following, and (c) the acute danger of invasion and political intervention by foreign troops.

Apart from the institution of ostracism, the only major reform that tradition agreed in attributing to Cleisthenes was the reorganization of the Athenian citizen body for government and administration. The result of the reforms was that what had been the centralized rule of an autocrat was replaced by a fresh set of man-made arrangements in which nobles and non-nobles co-operated. In view of the danger of a new autocracy, leadership was divided among elected officials: *there would be no head of state*, power would rotate. All Athenian citizens would participate in the decision-making process, *and none would be supreme*. The personal power and unpredictable will of an autocrat was replaced by the rule of common law; centralized justice dealt out by a ruler was replaced by people's courts; the defence of the state was entrusted to citizen hoplites, recruited through the demes, brigaded into tribal regiments, and commanded by *elected* generals.

At the time of crisis, when the revolution which had ousted the tyrants was itself in danger, the internal and external threats were closely connected, and both involved the deployment of armed force. Only the hoplites could protect Athens from invasion, and their deployment in a civil conflict would be decisive.

The mobilization of citizen power was a key to success in the internal, as well as the external, situation. Aristotle's account of the Cleisthenic reforms is mainly concerned with the reorganization of the citizen body for the purposes of government; reference to the new military structure comes only later (*AP* 22, see Section XXII(a), with note 5), giving the impression that the military reorganization came as an incidental consequence of the new civic arrangements. But the impression may be merely a consequence of Aristotle's loose arrangement of his material. It is possible that military considerations were of paramount importance in the reorganization. This view has recently gained support from an important contribution by P. Siewert (*Die Trittyen Attikes und die Heeresreform des Kleisthenes*, Munich 1982) who suggested that it was a principle of Cleisthenes' reorganization that the demes of each *trittys* should as far as possible be located along lines of communication with Athens city in order to facilitate the mobilization of the hoplites.

For further reading see *HAC*, 132–58; C. W. J. Eliot, 'Kleisthenes and the creation of the ten phylai', *Phoenix* 22, 1968, 3–17; J. S. Traill, *The Political Organisation of Attica*, Hesperia Sup. 14, 1975; D. M. Lewis, 'Cleisthenes and Attica', *Historia* 12, 1963, 22–40.

5. In the classical period the naucraries no longer existed; and the meaning of the term, and the functions of the magistracy, were in doubt. Herodotus, writing of events in the seventh century, described the presidents of the naucraries as the supreme magistrates at Athens (see Section I(a)). In pre-Solonian Athens, according to Aristotle (*AP* 8) (see Section VIII(a)) the four tribes had each been divided into three *trittyes*; each *trittys* had included twelve naucraries; their officials were concerned with levies and expenditures. The form of the word (*naukleros* = a ship's master) suggests that the duties attached to the magistracy were connected with the provision of ships, and this was believed by ancient scholars. But this belief, generally accepted by modern historians, is not supported by Aristotle's vague comment, in this passage, that the new officials, the demarchs or headmen of the demes, took over the duties of the naucrari; for, in the classical period at least, the demarchs were not concerned with ships. The confusion is increased by a remark by one of the earliest Athenian historians, Cleidemus, writing in the mid-fourth century, that, so far from replacing the naucrary organization, Cleisthenes actually divided Attica into fifty naucraries (*FGH* 323 F 8). With the organization of the demes we are on much firmer ground. The country demes comprised clusters of population, in most cases with a traditional organization structure, and supplied the territorial and demographic units on which the tribal reform was based. Perhaps the city demes were created by Cleisthenes, as part of his master plan, in an attempt to equalize them in voting power. The record of deme members was kept by the demarchs; when a member moved away from the deme, he retained his membership, as did his descendants after him. For administrative purposes the deme membership of citizens, hence their distribution for policitcal purposes, was frozen in the pattern established in the year of the reform (508–507 BC). As time passed and population shifted around, in particular from rural to urban areas, the gap widened between the theoretical distribution of citizens, and their actual location. A system based orginally on the place of residence of the citizens became later a system based partly on tradition.

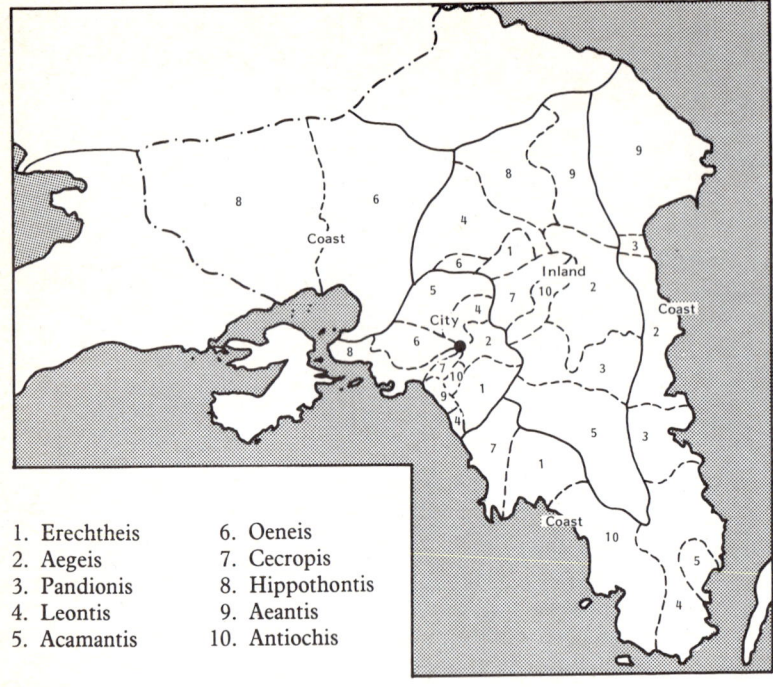

1. Erechtheis
2. Aegeis
3. Pandionis
4. Leontis
5. Acamantis
6. Oeneis
7. Cecropis
8. Hippothontis
9. Aeantis
10. Antiochis

The tribe and *trittys* organization of fifth-century Attica

The sketch illustrates the general pattern of the reorganization: there is dispute about the details.

XXII THE LAW ON OSTRACISM

(a) After these reforms had been carried out,[1] the constitution became much more like that of a democracy than the constitution of Solon had been. The sequence of events was that the tyranny had consigned to oblivion the laws of Solon, as they had fallen into disuse,[2] and Cleisthenes enacted new laws with an eye to popular support. Among them was the law on ostracism.[3] First of all, four years[4] after the settlement, in the archonship of Hermocrion, they instituted for the Council of Five Hundred the oath which is still in use. Then later, they began to select the generals by tribes, one from each tribe, but the commander of the whole army was the polemarch.[5] Eleven years later, in the archonship of Phainippus, they won the battle of Marathon. Two years after that battle, when the demos was full of confidence, the first use was made of the law on ostracism; it had originally been enacted through suspicion of men in high places, because of Peisistratus, who had himself been a popular leader and a general, and had made himself tyrant. The first person to be ostracized was one of his relatives, named Hipparchus, son of Charmus, of the Kollytos deme; and it was because of him in particular that Cleisthenes had made the law, wanting to drive him out of the country.[6] With the tolerance normal in the democratic style, the Athenians had permitted the friends of the tyrants to go on living in Athens unless they had personally been guilty of offences during the riots: and the leader and champion of these people was Hipparchus. So, immediately afterwards, in the following year, in the archonship of Telesinus, for the first time since the tyranny, they chose by lot the nine archons on a tribal basis from a list of 500 who had previously been selected by the members of demes. Before that date all the archons had been voted upon.[7] And Megacles, Hippocrates' son, of the deme Alopeke, was ostracized. So for three years they went on ostracizing the tyrant's friends, who were the very people at whom the law had been aimed. Then from the fourth year onwards it was used generally to get rid of anybody who was thought to be getting too powerful. The first victim of the ostracism law who had nothing to do with the tyranny was Xanthippus, Ariphron's son.

Aristotle, AP 22.1–5

(b) Of him [Hipparchus, son of Charmus] Androtion says, in the second book, that he was a relative of the tyrant Peisistratus, and was the first man to be ostracized, as the law about ostracism had just then been passed, and because of the suspicion with which Peisistratus' followers were regarded; for he had been a demagogue and a general, and had made himself tyrant.

Harpocration (FGH 324 F 6)

(c) Cleisthenes introduced the law about ostracism into Athens – the law was as follows. The custom was for the council[8] to consider for a few days, then to write down on *ostraka* (potsherds) the name of whichever of the citizens had to be exiled, and to cast these sherds into the council enclosure. Whoever had more than 200 sherds cast against him should be exiled for ten years, without loss of his farm income. Later on it was resolved by the demos that the law should be that the man to be exiled had to have over 6000 sherds cast against him.

Vaticanus Graecus 1144, fol. 222

(d) Before the eighth prytany[9] the demos would hold a preliminary vote whether to take the decision to hold an ostracism. When they decided to do so, the agora was fenced around with timbers, and ten entrances were left, through which men entered, tribe by tribe, and deposited their sherds, keeping the written side face downwards. The nine archons and the council presided. After the count had been taken, whoever scored the highest number, and at least 6000, was bound to settle all his private commitments within ten days, and to quit Athens for ten years (later on, the period was shortened to five years); he was to receive the fruits of his property,[10] but not to pass beyond Geraestus, the promontory of Euboea.

Philochorus (FGH 328 F 30)

(e) The procedure was, in brief, as follows. Each man took an *ostrakon* and on it wrote [the name of] that citizen whom he wished to banish, and took it to a place in the agora that had been encircled with a fence. First of all, the archons counted the sum total of sherds; for, if the voters should be less than 6000, the ostracism was null and void. They then put each of the names in a separate pile, and the one who had scored highest they proclaimed banished for ten years, though receiving the fruits of his own property.

Plutarch, Aristeides 7.4

---

1. Referring to the tribal reform (see Section XXI).
2. An apparent contradiction to the tradition that during the tyranny the legal arrangements functioned unchanged (see Section XIV n.4).
3. This whole chapter seems compressed and confused. After mentioning the law on ostracism Aristotle fills in the time interval, until (as he believed) it was first used, with other developments.
4. According to Aristotle's reckoning, this should place the law on ostracism in the year 504–503. But a few lines later Aristotle dates the adoption of the new council oath and the new method of selecting generals to eleven years before the battle of Marathon, that is, to the year 501–500 BC; furthermore the archon for the year 504–503 was not, as far as we know, Hermocrion, but Acestorides. It appears that either Aristotle himself, or a later copyist, had made a mistake in the date, and, to 'correct' the chronology, editors of the text have accepted an emendation, 'in the *eighth* year', rather than 'in the *fifth* year'; the law on ostracism, the new oath, and the new method of selecting generals are all believed to have taken place in 501–500, in the archonship of Hermocrion. (But see note 6 below.) It is these three measures which, in Aristotle's view, made Athens much more democratic. For the tribal reform and the new Council of Five Hundred merely established new machinery of administration, and in themselves they would not necessarily have been more proof against manipulation by a tyrant, or by

an aristocracy, than the Solonian constitution had been.

For a discussion of the problem of the chronology see F. Shachermeyer, *Klio* 25, 1932, 347; T. J. Cadoux, *JHS* 68, 1948, 115–19; *HAC*, Appendix VII.

5. It is notable that Aristotle does not specifically ascribe the authorship of the two measures to Cleisthenes, but he is specific about assigning the law on ostracism to him. It is the more notable because of the almost inexplicable delay which is alleged to have occurred between the passing of the law on ostracism and its first employment. The selection of generals was a particularly sensitive issue, for the command of troops had been the weapon by which a tyrant had secured power, both at Athens and elsewhere. Previously army commanders had been appointed for specific campaigns, as, it is thought, Peisistratus had been appointed to lead troops against Megara in the struggle for Salamis. The innovation introduced at this time involved a routine and changing command structure authorized by the assembly after selection through the new tribes. The new system seems to have worked well both in a military sense, and from the point of view of civic control over the military. We see the new system of command at work in Herodotus' account of the battle of Marathon in 490 BC. (See note 7 below.)

6. Aristotle's statement, that the law on ostracism was passed soon after the end of the tyranny but was not used until 488–487, contradicts Androtion's remark (see (b) above) that the law was enacted about the time when it was first used. There is an obvious improbability in the notion that a law was passed with a particular victim in mind, but that twenty years elapsed before the law was ever used, and that the victim was, after all, the very person at whom the law had been aimed a generation earlier. The force of the improbability, plus the witness of Androtion, have inclined many historians to doubt the accuracy of Aristotle's account. Aristotle used Androtion as a source elesewhere, and the close resemblance in language between the two versions suggests that Aristotle was in fact following him here; but, on the question of the dating and authorship of the law, Aristotle chose to disagree with his source. There was no disagreement between them about the identity of the first victim of the law; the question that interested historians was, 'Who was the real founder of Athenian democracy?' (And ostracism was one of its more controversial institutions.) The dating of the law depended on its authorship: if the law was passed in 488, then it was almost certainly *not* the work of Cleisthenes. The Athenian tradition was evidently divided as to the authorship of the law. Androtion, who was prepared to minimize the radical aspects of Solon's reforms (see Section V(c) note) and to blame the excesses of the democracy on later demagogues, was likely to have preferred to excuse Cleisthenes from responsibility for ostracism, which had, when he wrote, long been discredited. If in fact the first victim of ostracism was Hipparchus, in 487, it could be inferred that the law had only recently been passed, and Cleisthenes could not have been responsible. This is the tradition accepted by Androtion and rejected by Aristotle. But why in fact was the controversy not settled by consulting the actual law? Presumably because no copy of the law was available, the controversy was carried on through inference. One document, however, *was* available to throw light on the discussion. In 481–480, at the height of Athenian peril during the Persian war, a decree was passed recalling from exile all current victims of ostracism, that is, all those ostracized since 491–490; the names were listed on the decree, and, it seems, Hipparchus (ostracized 487)

stood at the head. Thus he became the first victim attested in contemporary records, and was consequently regarded as the first victim ever. Androtion's belief, that the law on ostracism had not long preceded its first use, was a natural inference, and one that acquitted Cleisthenes of responsibility for the law. Aristotle however believed that Cleisthenes had played a decisive part in the development of Athenian democratic institutions, had been a strong opponent of tyranny, and had devised the law against would-be tyrants. Aristotle accepted the idea that Hipparchus was the first victim, but preferred the tradition that ascribed the law to Cleisthenes, in spite of the delay in its implementation. To explain the awkward delay, he therefore cited the self-confidence engendered in the Athenians by their victory at Marathon, and their tolerance in allowing friends of the tyrants to continue living in Athens.

7. The new method of selecting the archons is dated to the year 487–486 by Aristotle, both by the archon-year and by the fact that it was in the year following the ostracism of Hipparchus. The account leaves a good deal unsaid, and has aroused considerable controversy. Aristotle has already described how, in his view, the archons were selected in the Solonian constitution, and it is, like the method used after 487, a mixture of election followed by sortition; a short list of forty was chosen, and from this list nine were chosen by drawing lots (*AP* 8; Section VIII(a) n.4). In the present passage he writes that, before 487, the archons had been *elected*. Aristotle's account can be made consistent by supposing that during the tyranny the use of lot for the selection of archons was discontinued, for the selection was rigged, if we rightly understand Thucydides 6.54 (Section XVI(b)); then, after the tyranny fell, the archons were chosen by direct election until 487, when the new system began, reverting to the combined method of election plus sortition. According to this argument, in 490 BC the polemarch should have been directly elected. But in describing the arrangements at the battle of Marathon, Herodotus says specifically (6.109) that the polemarch Callimachus had obtained his office 'by the bean' (i.e. by the luck of the draw). The comment has caused speculation that in 490 BC, that is *before* the reform, the archons were already being appointed by a process including sortition. But Herodotus' language suggests that it was the office of polemarch, rather than that of archon, that had been balloted, that is, that the nine archons had in fact been elected by the assembly, and only then did they draw lots for the actual offices they would hold. The system had merit if an intention of the Cleisthenic reforms was to reduce the opportunities in the system for any individual to establish himself in a seat of particular power; and one recalls that the road to tyranny had run through the position of military commander. On the other hand the luck of the draw is a risky way of selecting the man to lead an army into battle. How the system worked (or how Herodotus supposed it worked) is seen in his narrative about the battle of Marathon. The polemarch holds the position of honour as commander-in-chief, but the tactical command is in the hands of the generals (*strategoi*). During the fifth century the position of the generals in the state became stronger, while that of the archons weakened, until the duties of the polemarch became merely ceremonial; the question arises whether the change in 487 was a deliberate attempt to weaken the authority of the archonship in favour of the *strategia*. Much of the argument in favour of this view rests on the assumption that changes in the division of power in a state arise from changes

in the institutional arrangements. But experience often suggests the reverse: institutional change often simply recognizes actual changes in the distribution of power. When Athens embarked upon the dangerous course of overseas adventures, the men who commanded task forces and warships needed qualifications, and acquired a mystique, greater than that accorded to other magistrates. As Athens developed her military and naval potential generals became the chief magistrates in the state, and the former chief magistracy, the archonship, became a civic job which could safely be entrusted to an officer in whose selection chance played a part. This may have been the reason why Athens adopted, or returned to, the process of selection in 487 BC. For discussion on this issue, see E. Badian, 'Archons and strategoi', *Antichthon* 5, 1971, 1–34.

8. The Vatican manuscript (c), by an unknown hand, and dating from the fifteenth century AD, describes the procedure for ostracism in a way that disagrees radically with other accounts. The source of the tradition followed by the writer is unknown, and the account is generally written off by modern historians as a mere curiosity. But the account has some internal consistency which calls for examination of its standing. It supposes that ostracism, as it was known in the fifth century, was preceded by an earlier form of banishment exercised by the council. The number 200, as the minimum needed to cause the victim to be banished, is consistent with the idea that the procedure was carried out in the Solonian Council of Four Hundred, that is, that a mere majority was needed. It would also be consistent with the theory that Cleisthenes brought forward his ostracism bill in 510 BC, in the period of his tussle with Isagoras, when the Solonian constitution was still in force, with the intention of putting the procedure in the hands of the council; and that the transfer of control over ostracism to the assembly was a later change. The account in this manuscript would reconcile two apparently contradictory traditions, that Cleisthenes was the author of the ostracism law, and that its first use (by the *assembly*) was much later. One reason for distrusting the account is that it is probably wrong about the minimal number of 6000 sherds required to be cast against the victim (see note 9 below); and if it is wrong on this point, its reliability becomes questionable on other points too. For comment see R. Develin, 'Cleisthenes and ostracism', *Antichthon* 11, 1977, 10–21.

9. The prytany was the tenth part of the year (the 'month') during which each of the ten tribal delegations of 500 men 'presided', that is, was in constant session at Athens, sitting as a subcommittee of the council with authority to act in its name. The procedure for conducting an ostracism was as follows. In the sixth prytany the assembly, without debate, took a vote on the question whether to hold an ostracism that year. If the decision was in the affirmative, the actual ostracism was held in the agora during the eighth prytany. Voters entered the enclosed space through ten gates, according to tribe, so that their eligibility to vote could be checked. Each voter wrote down on a sherd the name of the person whom he judged to be most deserving of the sentence of exile. The victim of this reverse-popularity contest who achieved the highest score was then exiled from Attica without loss of property or income for ten years. There is a conflict in the sources about whether, in fact, 6000 was the minimum total number of sherds cast necessary to *make an ostracism valid*, or whether the 'successful' victim had to have 6000 sherds *cast against him*. The view expressed by Plutarch, that

unless 6000 votes were cast the ostracism was null and void (victimless), is the one that is generally accepted. The number 6000 occurs elsewhere as the requred quorum for the treatment of other business by the assembly, and for the number of jurors who, in certain cases, sat as a court representing the whole demos. Bearing in mind that the total attendance was unlikely to be very much higher than 6000, had it been the minimal number of votes cast against an individual necessary to secure his exile, it seems unlikely that there would ever have been any victims, as a wide scatter of votes could be expected against the unlimited range of potential victims. Philochoros is therefore regarded as mistaken in his view that 6000 was the number of votes necessary against the victim (an error shared with the Vatican codex), and also in his belief that the period of exile was subsequently shortened to five years.

10. An interesting feature of the institution is the proviso that the victim retained the rights to the fruits of his property while in exile. It is far from clear how the actual fruits could be transferred to him when he was abroad, nor does it seem likely that in the time of Cleisthenes a transfer of money income in lieu could have been contemplated as a normal thing. Furthermore, ownership of land was regarded as vested in the family, not in the individual member of a family. In trying to understand how the system actually worked, we are constantly reminded how little we really know of conditions at the time. In this case we may guess that the wording of the law was changed several times in the course of the period when the law was in force (until the ostracism of Hyperbolus in 417 BC), and that the wording appropriate to the later period was attached by the Attic historians to the original law of Cleisthenes. Modern archaeology has discovered solid evidence of the institution of ostracism. More than 16,000 inscribed potsherds have so far been discovered, carrying the names of well over a hundred intended victims; usually only the name appears, occasionally accompanied by vivid comments.[1] After counting, the collected sherds cast against a particular candidate were apparently dumped, and some such dumps have been discovered. An interesting suspicion has been voiced, namely that numbers of sherds were inscribed by the same hands; if the suspicion is justified, it may be taken as evidence about the spread of literacy among the citizens of Athens, or it may suggest corruption in the voting process.

The institution of ostracism has often been highly praised as an instance of a people's democracy in action. From the point of view of human rights, it may be regarded as surprising that so little criticism has been expressed, either in ancient times or by modern historians, of a legal measure which could award a man ten years' exile without any offence being proved, or even alleged, against him.

For further reading on the institution and working of ostracism, see *HAC*, 159–66; *GHI*, no. 21; Vanderpool, *Ostracism at Athens*; Thomsen, *The Origin of Ostracism*.

---

[1] A unique example is a sherd on which a voter has expressed his views on a candidate in a verse couplet, which reads:

This sherd says that Xanthippus son of Ariphron
is the biggest rascal of all the damned leaders.

XXIII ATHENS AT WAR WITH HER NEIGHBOURS

(a) Cleomenes realized that he had been insulted by the Athenians in word
and deed, and collected an army from the whole Peloponnese without
specifying its objective. His intention was to make the Athenian demos
pay for its actions, and to set up Isagoras as tyrant there, for the latter
had come out of the Acropolis with him.[1] Cleomenes crossed into
Eleusis with a large force, and the Boeotians, in a concerted strategy,
took Oenoe and Hysiae, the frontier townships in Attica, while the
Chalcidians, moving in on the other front, laid waste to several places
in Attica.[2] The Athenians were encircled, but they put off dealing with
the Boeotians and Chalcidians until later, and struck at the
Peloponnesians, who were at Eleusis. But when the two forces were
about to engage, the Corinthian contingent was the first to break ranks;
reasoning that the cause they were supporting was in the wrong, they
turned, and withdrew from the action. Their example was followed
by Ariston's son Demaratus, himself a Spartan king, who had shared
the leadership of the force from Lacedaemon, and hitherto had not been
in conflict with Cleomenes. . . . When the rest of the allies at Eleusis
saw that the Spartan kings were divided and the Corinthians were
breaking ranks, they also took action to withdraw. . . . When the
expeditionary force had thus ingloriously broken up, the Athenians
decided to strike back, and first moved in upon the Chalcidians. The
Boeotians came up to the river Euripus to help the Chalcidians and,
seeing the Boeotians, the Athenians decided to assault them first. The
Athenians closed in upon them, and were soon on top: they dealt out
great slaughter, and took 700 prisoners. On the same day the Athenians
crossed into Euboea and were in action against the Chalcidians. Against
them too they were victorious, and left 4000 Athenian settlers on the
land of the Horse-breeders, as the rich men of Chalcis were called.[3]
Those of them that they took prisoner, they held under close arrest
and fettered, together with the Boeotian prisoners. In the course of time
they were ransomed for two minas each. But the fetters in which they
had been confined were hung up on the Acropolis, and they are still
to be seen there in my time, hanging from walls scorched by the Persian
conflagration, and opposite the chapel that faces west. The Athenians
offered up a tenth part of the ransom as a dedication, in the form of
a bronze chariot. It is the first thing you see on the left hand as you
pass into the Great Porch on the Acropolis. On it is written the following

inscription:

> BY THEIR DEEDS IN WAR THE SONS OF THE ATHENIANS
> BROUGHT LOW THE COMPANIES OF BOEOTIANS AND CHALCIDIANS
> IN SOMBRE CHAINS OF IRON THEY BROKE THEIR SPIRIT
> AND THIS, THEIR CHARIOT, THE TITHE, SET UP FOR PALLAS
> ATHENA.[4]

Now the Athenians grew in strength, an object lesson that, not in one but in every respect, political equality is a great thing. For while they were living under a tyranny the Athenians had proved less warlike than any of their neighbours, but once they got rid of the tyrants they were by far the best. It proves that while they were held down, they had no stomach for it, like slaves working for a master, but once they were free, every one of them was keen to get on with the job.

Herodotus 5.74–8

(b) There are two Athenian dedications from a tithe of spoils – a bronze statue of Athena by Pheidias from the Persian landing at Marathon, and a bronze chariot from Boeotia and from Chalcis in Euboea.

Pausanias 1.28

---

1. See Section XX (a) n. 9. Herodotus credits the Spartans with two attempts to restore tyranny at Athens. After the failure of the attempt to set up Isagoras, which is portrayed as part of a personal vendetta on Cleomenes' part, they are said to have invited Hippias to return from his place of exile at Sigeum, and to have urged their allies to join in a crusade to restore him, the aim being to keep Athens weak, and vulnerable to Spartan pressure. The story seems strangely at odds with the general reputation of Sparta as the destroyer of tyrants in Greece. In the pages of Herodotus the brilliant and eccentric career of Cleomenes and his tragic death mark him out as a doomed hero, and the saga of his life bears touches of romantic myth which make it hard to evaluate as a factual account.
2. 'The situation is a suspiciously exact anticipation of the situation about 446 BC, and the tactics of the Athenians are prophetic' (Macan, *Herodotus IV-VI*, vol. 1). It is not, after all, so improbable that a situation involving frontier clashes with neighbours should be repeated, but the details of the action which took place in 446, when Herodotus was already preparing his great work, may have affected his retrospect of the earlier action.
3. It is difficult to accept the account as it stands, for the official planting of an overseas settlement by the Athenian state was a matter of some ceremony and prior organization. The system of planting cleruchies on confiscated land belongs to the period of Athenian imperialism in the fifth century; the settlement here described must have been a much more improvised land grab, if it is true. There is again a (perhaps) suspicious resemblance in the 506 situation to that which occurred in the mid-fifth century, when the Athenian admiral Tolmides

established a cleruchy on Euboea (Pausanias 1.27.6).

4. Herodotus copied the verses from the base on which the bronze chariot was mounted; and the accuracy of his reporting can be checked from the finds of archaeologists. Fragments of the base which he saw have been recovered, and also fragments from an earlier base, erected in the sixth century and presumably vandalized during the Persian occupation of 480–479. In the mid-fifth century the monument was evidently restored, using a marble base, whereas the original had been of limestone; the dating of the two bases is indicated by the style of lettering. Whereas the order of the verses on the later monument corresponds with the order which Herodotus reproduced, on the earlier base the order is transposed; the verses which in Herodotus and the later plinth are numbered 1, 2, 3, 4, on the earlier plinth read 3, 4, 1, 2, which was apparently the original form. Herodotus states that the monument was sited near the entrance to the Acropolis, although the fetters were some distance away, hanging on the temple wall (the old temple of Athena, which predated the classical temple). Pausanias, however, by his description (b) implies that the monument he saw was near to the great statue of Athena Promachos which stood facing the great entrance, and at some distance from it. It has therefore been suggested that the original site of the monument was near the statue, as Pausanias wrote, but that the chariot was removed or destroyed during the Persian occupation. The new monument from the fifth century was set up near the entrance, where Herodotus saw it, then later it was moved back to the original site, where it was later seen by Pausanias. (See *GHI*, no. 15.)

BIBLIOGRAPHY

Andrews, A. *The Greek Tyrants*. London 1956.
— *The Greeks*. London 1967.
Austin, M. M. and Vidal, Naquet P. *Economic and Social History of Ancient Greece*. London 1977.
Berve, H. *Die Tyrannis bei den Griechen*. Munich 1967.
Boardman, J. and Hammond, N. G. L. *The Cambridge Ancient History*. 2nd edn, vol. III, 3. Cambridge 1982.
Burn, A. R. *The Lyric Age of Greece*. London 1960.
Day, J. and Chambers, M. *Aristotle's History of Athenian Democracy*. Berkeley 1962.
De Sanctis, G. *Atthis: Storia della Repubblica Ateniense*. Turin 1912.
Ehrenberg, V. *The Greek State*. London 1963.
— *From Solon to Socrates*. London 1973.
Eliot, C. W. *The Coastal Demes of Attica*. Toronto 1962.
Finley, M. I. *Studies in Land and Credit in Ancient Athens*. New Brunswick 1952.
— *Democracy Ancient and Modern*. London 1973.
— *The Use and Abuse of History*. London 1975.
— *Politics in the Ancient World*. Cambridge 1983.
Fornara, C. W. *Archaic Times to the End of the Peloponnesian War*. Cambridge 1983.
Forrest, W. G. *The Emergence of Greek Democracy*. London 1966.
Freeman, K. *The Work and Life of Solon*. Cardiff 1926.
French, A. *Growth of the Athenian Economy*. London 1964.
Fuks, A. *The Ancestral Constitution*. London 1953.
Gomme, A. W. *A Historical Commentary on Thucydides*, vol. 1. Oxford 1945.
Hammond, N. G. L. *History of Greece*. Oxford 1967.
— *Studies in Greek History*. Oxford 1971.
Harrison, A. R. W. *The Law of Athens*. Oxford 1968–71.
Hignett, C. *A History of the Athenian Constitution*. Oxford 1952.
Hill, I. T. *The Ancient City of Athens*. London 1953.
Hopper, R. J. *The Acropolis*. London 1971.
— *The Early Greeks*. London 1976.
Jacoby, F. *Die Fragmente der griechischen Historiker*. Leiden 1940–58.
— *Atthis*. Oxford 1949.
Jeffery, L. H. *The Local Scripts of Archaic Greece*. Oxford 1961.
— *Archaic Greece, the City-states*. London 1976.
Kraay, C. M. and Hirmer, J. *Greek Coins*. London 1966.
Linforth, I. M. *Solon the Athenian*. Berkeley 1919.
Macan, R. W. *Herodotus*. London 1895, 1908.
Meiggs, R. and Lewis, D. *Greek Historical Inscriptions*. Oxford 1969.
Moore, J. M. *Aristotle and Xenophon on Democracy and Oligarchy*. London 1975.
Mossé, C. *La Tyrannie dans la Grèce antique*. Paris 1969.
Murray, O. *Early Greece*. London 1980.
Ostwald, M. *Nomos and the Beginnings of Athenian Democracy*. Oxford 1969.
Pearson, L. *The Local Historians of Attica*. Philadelphia 1942.
Rhodes, P. J. *The Athenian Boule*. Oxford 1972.

— *Commentary on the Aristotelian Athenaion Politeia*. Oxford 1981.
— *Aristotle, the Athenian Constitution*. London 1984.
Ruschenbusch, E. *Solonos Nomoi*. Wiesbaden 1966.
Sealey, R. *Essays in Greek Politics*. New York 1967.
— *History of the Greek City-states*. Berkeley 1976.
Thomsen, R. *Eisphora*. Copenhagen 1964.
— *The Origin of Ostracism*. Copenhagen 1972.
Vanderpool, E. *Ostracism at Athens*. Cincinnati 1970.
Wade-Grey, H. T. *Essays in Greek History*. Oxford 1958.
Woodhead, A. G. *The Study of Greek Inscriptions*. Cambridge 1959.
Woodhouse, W. J. *Solon the Liberator*. Oxford 1938.

INDEX